PLAYING
WITH THE
BIG BOYS

PLAYING
WITH THE
BIG BOYS

A WOMAN'S GUIDE TO POKER

LAURA A. VAN VLEET AND G. L. NORRIS

BARNES & NOBLE BOOKS
NEW YORK

Published by MJF Books
Fine Communications
322 Eighth Avenue
New York, NY 10001

Playing with the Big Boys
LC Control Number 2004104112
ISBN 1-56731-680-8

Manufactured in the United States of America on acid-free paper ∞

MJF Books and the MJF colophon are trademarks of Fine Creative
Media, Inc.

QM   10   9   8   7   6   5   4   3   2   1

Men do it. Boys do it. Brothers and cousins and fathers and uncles, and whole college fraternities do it. Even cigar-smoking velvet dogs do it.

For many women, *it* remains something of a mystery, a closed brotherhood of time-honored codes and undeniable fun, complete with all the rituals of a secret society, a gathering of menfolk who meet around kitchen tables and in smoke-filled rooms all across America. Some members convene electronically via their home computers, or amid the bright lights of towns like Las Vegas and

Atlantic City to compete in high-stakes tournaments that pit their skills against other hardcore aficionados.

The *it* is a little thing the guys like to call Poker, and for many men, it's hands-off, ladies!

The closest most women ever get to a deck of cards is in college drinking games, or in safe, 'feminine' pursuits like Whist or Bridge. My introduction to Poker came on a frigid Thanksgiving afternoon when a group of friends and I sat around the house gorged and contemplating another slice of pumpkin pie following a huge meal complete with all the trimmings. These mostly-male friends, tired of watching football and too sated to stroll through the woods with us Goddesses who realized a brisk walk would shake off our sluggishness, retired to the kitchen table with a deck of cards and cups of fresh, hot coffee.

We returned to the house some time later and were greeted by the sound of laughter, wondering just what all the fun was about. Before that day, the idea of playing cards was something that only the men in my family had previously indulged in. As we helped ourselves to coffee, and the inevitable taunts from our male friends began, I remembered all those other nights from my youth when cards were dealt and spirited conversations ensued in a room I was not allowed to enter. Somewhere between recalling that 'Girls don't play cards,' and hearing my current friends tease 'You think you're good enough to win against us?' it all set in. It wasn't that I really hated the game of Poker; my contempt for it came from the fact I'd never been invited to join in as both a respected and feared equal. That was all about to change.

Never one to walk away from a challenge, I pulled up a chair. Revived by the walk, I was determined to show my male friends that not only could a woman hold her own at the Poker table, she could also beat them at their own game.

Call it beginner's luck, but beat them, I did.

We played on for hours that stretched deep into the night, joking and laughing, and having more fun than I ever had before in my life. Not only did I gain an understanding of Poker, I made a vow to master it, for that night, I became what I now lovingly refer to as a Poker Goddess.

The book you hold is the result of that promise, a practical and spirited handbook written for other hopeful Poker Goddesses everywhere who want to share in the fun that the guys have been keeping all to themselves. Ladies new to this strange and wonderful world will notice straight away the level of machismo that dominates Poker, down to the names of the games themselves: 5-Card Stud, 7-Card Stud, Grandfather, Football, Baseball, and Indian Poker. Even the Wild Card bonanza called 52 is oft-times referred to in many circles as *Balls* (I need not further explain the symbolism there). We have taken these games, demystified them, and redefined them in an easy to follow manner, all with a decidedly feminine twist.

With this book, we will also hopefully put many myths to rest, the first and foremost of which is that only men are capable of competing and winning at card games.

Yes, forget all that you've been previously told.

Real women do play Poker!

So gather the company of some great female friends, open a bottle of wine or put on the tea and coffee, pony up to the table with your spare change, and prepare to deal the cards.

Ladies, you're about to have the time of your lives!

A Brief History of Poker

A modern deck of two-dollar playing cards owes its beginning to an ancient dynasty in China over a thousand years ago — the first recorded use hails all the way back to the 10th Century and the invention of games that involved the shuffling and dealing of little paper 'dominos.' Elegant, rectangular hand-painted decks of cards with four different 'suits' sprung up in the Moslem world soon after, used in a game the Persians called 'Âs Nas.' These early decks of cards were highly prized by Europeans in the 1300's, and due to their uniqueness and scarcity, owning them became something of a status symbol since only the wealthy could afford to buy them.

All that changed in the late 14th Century with the invention of woodcuts, an early form of printing using blocks of tooled wood, ink, and paper. Thanks to the French, all of Europe was soon deluged by a case of mass-marketed 52 Pickup!

The French are also responsible for endowing modern playing cards with the four familiar suits we all have come to recognize: Clubs, Diamonds, Spades, and Hearts. At one time in centuries past, the French designed each King card in the deck to represent a famous historical figure: the King of Spades was King David from the Holy Bible, the King of Clubs was Alexander the Great, the King of Hearts, Charlemagne, and the King of Diamonds was Julius Ceasar.

Playing card games with these mass-marketed decks became something of a craze in England, then in the British Colonies in the New World. Americans began making their own version of playing cards at the onset of the 1800's, improving on what had come before. Whereas the French cards were printed with definite tops and bottoms to them, American cards adopted a two-headed direction, effectively cutting out the hassle of constantly having to right the cards to all face one way after they'd been dealt. Along with the double-headed design came rounded corners on the cards to cut down on wear and tear, and varnished surfaces, meaning a deck of cards lived a lot longer in the New World than its predecessors in Europe.

The game of Poker itself owes its origins to the Germans, who developed a bluffing game they called *Pochen*. Those industrious French, purveyors of such wondrous delights as eclairs, fried potatoes, and the mayonnaise food groups, furthered Poker's evolution by developing their own version, which they called *Poque*. That variation immigrated to New Orleans in the young United States, where it evolved into the game of Poker we all know today.

The first recorded mention of our version of the game hails back to the 1830's, when the name became official and the lure of playing cards competitively caught fire on riverboats up and down the Mississippi and Ohio Rivers before traveling east with the railroad. Given the raw machismo of the time, it's easy to understand how Poker's reputation as a man's game evolved. Poker was played by troops on both sides of the American Civil War, who added the rule about the drawing of cards to help improve a player's Hand. In keeping with the theme of a time when 'Men were Men,' Stud Poker was also created.

Along with these changes came another significant difference in the Americanized version of playing cards: the addition of the Joker to the deck circa 1870. Leave it to a bunch of guys to sneak a couple of Stooges into the mix! The Joker cards often come into play as Wild Cards in several variations of Poker, though their original design was to promote commercial advertising — the first billboards!

Out of the purest forms of Poker, a plethora of other fun and exciting card games were created, many of which will be covered in the chapters ahead. Remember that when you pick up a deck of cards, you are holding history in your hands — as well as the potential for a great deal of fun. Many happy memories have been born around Poker tables. May we create some and add to that rich history together!

PLAYING
WITH THE
BIG BOYS

CHAPTER ONE

Deal the Cards!

THE BASICS

A standard deck of playing cards can be found ANYWHERE — in grocery stores, dollar stores, specialty game stores, and all-night convenience stores. You may have noticed that some versions come decorated with scantily clad vixens in provocative poses on the back. Fear not, girls. Somebody somewhere saw fit to level the playing field. My favorite deck of cards is graced by a few dozen construction workers, cops, fireman, and military guys, none of whom seem to know how to shave, all of which look quite swarthy and easy on the eyes. Meow!

THE DECK

A deck of playing cards, you'll learn, comes with 52 individual cards, 13 to a suit. The cards, in order, run: 2, 3, 4, 5, 6, 7, 8, 9, 10, Jack, Queen, King, and Ace.

Two suits come in red, two in black. Those suits are:

SPADES: Sort of an upside-down heart in the black half of the deck. ♠

CLUBS: Sometimes referred to as 'Puppy Pawprints' ♣

HEARTS: Half of the red suits, easy to recognize ♥

&

DIAMONDS: Also red, which in Poker can sometimes be a girl's best friend! ♦

The deck also contains two:

JOKERS: which in some cases can be used as Wild Cards.

A fresh deck of cards, newly unwrapped from its plastic, needs a little attention and modification before it is ready to be used in a game of cards. Take out the two Jokers and set them aside as you learn how to shuffle the cards.

SHUFFLING

Take the cards in your hands. Get a feel for them. Cut the deck in half, making sure to keep the backs and fronts going in the same direction, and begin shuffling them from one hand to the other to mix up the order of the cards. This is the first step to learning how to go to the next phase of shuffling.

Once you've given the cards a good tossing, cut the deck in half again. Set each half face-down on the table, side by side. Now try to imagine that one half of the deck is a stack of hundred dollar bills. The other half is made up of fifties. There's a fortune on the table, and you're about to cash in!

Take the top, right corner of the left deck and carefully bend it up, making sure not to permanently mar the cards. Now carefully do the same with the upper left side corner of the right deck. With both sides raised, scoot the two halves together and slowly release them into one another. The cards will flap down, like pages of a new book being quickly flipped through. Once the cards of both halves of the deck are metered together, scoop the whole deck back into one uniform pile and repeat the process.

A wonderful older woman I played many a hand of cards with invested in a 'Card Shuffler' — an encyclopedia-sized, battery-operated machine that took two halves of the deck and shuffled them together, depositing the finished product neatly in a plastic tray. This machine was loud and unreliable, and provided much more in the way of comic relief than as an alternative to efforts by human hands. That this lovely woman often seemed to draw the one card she needed to win the pot seemingly out of thin air had us convinced she either had a card shuffler built into her body, or one hidden discreetly under the flaps of her house dress!

The more one practices shuffling, the better and quicker one gets. My first few efforts at shuffling were awkward and messy, with cards flying and falling in all directions. Your maiden voyage will likely be the same! This is a right of passage that all new Poker players will encounter, but with the correct amount of moxie and repetition, you'll be cracking open that box of cards and shuffling them at warp speed — like the clickety-clack of somebody who can type 80 words per minute!

THE DEALER

She who holds the shuffled deck in her stunningly manicured hands is the all-powerful Queen of the card game (until, of course, she passes the deal to the next Goddess seated at the table). The Dealer determines which game is to be played — it's entirely her 'call.' The deal always begins to the left of the Dealer to that Goddess seated at her left. However, the player to the Dealer's right has the option of cutting the cards before they are dealt (this is not a requisite, just an option designed to ensure the cards have been fairly dealt). If she chooses to cut the deck, she takes hold of it at some point midway down, cuts the deck and places both halves side by side, then rejoins the deck by sliding the bottom half onto the top and merging them back together WITHOUT shuffling the cards further. That accomplished, the deck has been cleanly cut and is ready to be dealt! But before you do, there are one or two things you will need to know.

Like Morse Code and Macho-Tango-Delta-Bravo military codespeak, Poker has its own unique lingo. The most important ones are listed below to better help facilitate an appreciation and understanding of the rules, for when in Rome...

A GLOSSARY OF POKER TERMS

52 PICKUP: More of a pain than a game. When a deck of cards is dropped and scattered across the floor, and must then be retrieved and reshuffled, this is known as 52 Pickup.

ACTION: The amount of money placed into the pot at the beginning of each game.

ACTIVE PLAYER: A Poker Goddess who is still in the game.

ANTE: The amount of money each Goddess ponies into the pot before a new Hand begins.

BANKROLL: The sum total amount of money you bring to play with.

BET: Your wager.

BETTING LIMITS: The minimum and maximum limits the Dealer sets to wager on the game. For instance, the minimum Bet may be a dime, the maximum, a quarter (or can go much higher based on the size of your bankroll!).

BLUFF: A very naughty but delicious trick — a deception on the part of a player who convinces other Goddesses into believing her Hand is better than it actually is. She may have a crummy Hand, but bet with confidence in the hope of driving others into folding who have better Hands than she. She may also have her Bluff called and wind up with egg on her Poker Face!

BOARD: Community Cards dealt face-up at the center of the table for all players to see.

BOARDED: When you discard your Hand, it is considered dead. Those cards are then 'boarded' and can't be used again until the deck is shuffled.

BOAT: Another term for a Full House, a.k.a. a 'Full Boat.'

CALL: When a player matches the current bet on the table, she 'calls.'

CARD COUNTING: When one keeps an eye on which cards have been played since the shuffle. Best to be silent and discreet about it!

CARD SHARK: An expert on playing cards. Such a brutal man's term! I like to think of us more as being lovely 'Card Angel Fish.'

CATCH: The cards dealt to you to help better your Hand after the discard. Hopefully, your catch is a good one!

CHEATING: A no-no. Something beneath us. A reason to have your eyes scratched out!

CHECK: This is when a player opts to stay in the game without betting. If you check, you are waiving your interest to pay more into the Pot — though she to your right just may and you will then be asked to match the Bet or fold.

CUT: An action by the Dealer to divide the deck in two parts and invert them after they've been well-shuffled.

CUTTHROAT: A style of play where it's every Goddess for herself!

DEAL: To hand out cards during a card game.

DEALER: She who wields the cards.

DEUCE: Another name for the 2 cards.

DRAW: The second round of cards dealt in a Hand of Draw Poker.

EDGE: An advantage you have over another player.

FACE CARDS: The Jack, Queen, and King cards of any suit in the deck. They're the ones with faces!

FOLD: When a player decides to drop out of the Hand and boards their cards.

HAND: A Hand refers to the cards you hold in your hands after the cards get shuffled.

HIGH POKER: Standard Poker where High Hands win — as opposed to Lowball, where the crummiest Hand splits the Pot!

HIGH ROLLER: Someone who bets with gusto and wild abandon!

HIT: To draw another card in the game of Blackjack.

HOLDING YOUR OWN: To break even.

HOLE CARD: Any card dealt face-down to a player. Also known as a pocket card.

HONORS: Honors is an extra free chance to remain in some card games after a player has exhausted her ability to buy into the next round.

HOT: A player on a winning streak.

LIMIT: A fixed limit on how high a Bet can be raised throughout each round. Also refers to the maximum set on the size of a Pot should players declare a ceiling on how high they will allow the Pot to grow to.

LOW POKER: Commonly called Lowball. This is Poker when the player with the worst Hand splits the Pot with the best Hand!

MISDEAL: When the Dealer accidentally deals too many cards, or a card is unintentionally dealt face-up, the cards are boarded and re-dealt to ensure fairness to all.

NATURAL: In Blackjack, natural is a two-card Hand that

totals 21 (an Ace accompanied by a Face card or 10). Also refers to a pure Hand without the benefit of Wild Cards — a natural Straight or Flush.

ODDS: The probabilities of catching a certain grouping of cards or of winning the Hand.

OPEN: After a player bids, the Hand is considered open.

PASS: To decline betting.

POKER FACE: That lovely expression you wear as betting begins. You may look calm and composed. You may appear absolutely giddy with barely contained enthusiasm. Or you might just look glassy-eyed and rabid.

POKER GODDESS: You.

POT: The Pot is where money is gathered at the center of the table once players ante, bet, and raise. She who wins the Hand takes the Pot.

PROGRESSIVE: A version of pure Poker wherein at least a Pair of Jacks are needed to open the bidding. If no players have this minimum in their Hands, players ante to the Pot again and cards are dealt again, with the minimum opening Hand progressing up to a Pair of Queens. This continues to Kings and Aces unless a Pair of Jacks opens the bidding, then progresses back in order from Aces to Kings to Queens to Jacks until the Hand is finally opened.

RAISE: When a player matches a Bet, then increases the stakes to the other Goddesses. "I'll match your quarter and raise you a quarter!"

SHOWDOWN: Once the last round of betting concludes, the remaining active players must show their Hands to determine the winner.

SHUFFLE: When the Dealer mixes the cards up to prepare to hand them out.

STEAL: To win the Pot by bluffing on a bad hand. We have also jokingly referred to this act as taking a 'cheap one.'

THREE C'S: Champagne, Chocolate, and Cigars — some wonderful additions (in moderation, of course) to any friendly game of Poker.

TREY: Another name for the 3 card.

TRIPS: Another name for Three of a Kind.

WILD CARD: Any card, including the Jokers, which can be used as any other card to complete your Hand.

Are you picking up on the vibe? Itching to deal those cards and begin your rise to infamy as a master of the game? First, you will need to acquaint yourself with the Poker Hands themselves. The following chart rates each Hand in Poker, from highest to lowest.

POKER HANDS

♣ FIVE OF A KIND:

This Hand can only happen in a game when Wild Cards have been named (for instance: 5, 5, 5, 5, and a Wild Card, or 5, 5, 5, and two Wild Cards).

♦ ROYAL FLUSH:

A, K, Q, J, and 10 cards, all in the same suit (for instance: all Spades, all Hearts).

♥ STRAIGHT FLUSH:

Any five-card sequence in the same suit (for instance: 5, 6, 7, 8, 9 or 9, 10, J, Q, K. There is no 'going around the corner,' i.e. Q, K, A, 2, 3. An Ace can lead before a 2 or follow a K in sequence, not both).

♠ FOUR OF A KIND:

All four cards of the same index (for instance: 8, 8, 8, 8 or Q, Q, Q, Q).

♣ FULL HOUSE:

Three of a Kind combined with a Pair (for instance: J, J, J, 7, 7)

♦ FLUSH:

Any five cards of the same suit (for instance: the 2, 7, 10, K, and A of Diamonds)

♥ STRAIGHT:

Five cards running in sequence, though not in the same suit (for instance, 3, 4, 5, 6, 7 comprised of multiple suits).

♠ THREE OF A KIND:
Three cards of the same value (for instance: 10, 10, 10)

♣ TWO PAIR:
Two sets of two cards with similar values (for instance: 3, 3, K, K)

♦ PAIR:
Two cards of the same value (for instance, 4, 4)

♥ HIGH CARD:
One card with a higher value than another player's (for instance, K beats J)

TIE-BREAKERS

If two players tie each other by rank (say you each hold Flushes, Straights or Full Houses in your Hands), the following tie-breakers apply:

♣ Should two players each have Straight Flushes, Flushes, or Straights, the Highest Card that is part of the Hand determines who wins. If the Highest Card still results in a tie (for instance, you have an Ace high, and so does she), the next Highest Card determines the winner.

♦ If two players show a Full House, then the three Highest Cards in either Hand determines the winner.

♥ If two players have Three of a Kind in their Hands, the

highest ranking three determines the winner (for instance, your three Kings beats out her three Jacks).

♠ If two players each show two Pairs, the highest Pair determines the winner. Should both players each have a Pair of Aces, the player holding the next highest Pair in rank wins.

♣ If two players have a single matching Pair, the highest-ranking Pair wins. If this is a tie (you each have a Pair of 10's, say), the next highest ranking single card wins. For instance, you both have that Pair of 10's, but she's got a King card, you've got an Ace. You win.

♦ In an instance where nobody has drawn a Pair or above, the highest ranking card wins the Hand. If this yet yields a tie (High Card in two Hands is a King), then the next Highest Card determines the winner.

Kapeesh?

We have now covered all the basics save one, and in deference to the people I play cards with, to me this is the most important of all.

PLAYING FAIR

No good friendship is worth losing over a game of cards, and at this early point in your mastery of Poker, you will be pitting your skills against your friends. While it's okay to declare your cutthroat independence against your fellow Poker Goddesses, remember there is a code of honor that should be followed while trying to win their coffee money.

Never let another player see the cards in your hands when they are dealt down to you. Keep them shielded and raised vertically from all prying eyes. And by the same standard, never peek or pry at your neighbor's. Should she lower her Hand accidentally as spirited laughter consumes the group (because you will be having so much fun!), gently remind her that she is flashing the table.

When mistakes are made during play and you catch them, calmly explain to your fellow Goddesses that there's been an error. In a level voice, declare a misdeal, shuffle the cards, and deal them again. There is rarely any need to intentionally create a scene involving 52 Pickup because one friend innocently thinks she has the top Hand on the Poker table when in fact she has miscounted her cards!

Also, if given the temptation to cheat, fight it. Where's the joy in looking at a friend's cards when she excuses herself to the powder room? Half of the fun of playing Poker is the challenge to beat the odds, the not-knowing! Such behavior can ruin the excitement of meeting for recreational card games should such indiscretion be discovered. Do it in a Las Vegas casino, and it can get you jail time and an ugly orange jumpsuit!

Remember, this is all about having fun. It's about playing fair, even when you reach competitive levels like those we will discuss in later chapters, and winning without selling your soul along the way. Above all, it's about proving that a couple of Jills and their gal-pals have what it takes to beat a pair of Jacks any day of the week!

CHAPTER TWO

52 Pickup is not 'Real' Poker

A few final important notations must first be prefaced in anticipation of your first night of fun and card play. Once you and your fellow maidens are ready to go, who is to be your first Dealer? Who is the Goddess who will kick things off and start the gathering's activities?

THE OPENING DEAL

This is always determined by a cut of the deck.

Set your cards down central to all of you, and one at a time, cut the deck. Simply enough, the Goddess who wins the Highest Card wins the deal. The one holding that High Card is your first Dealer and she determines the first game you'll play.

HIGH/LOW

Remember that in Poker, the Ace cards are always high, and the 2's are always low.

STAKES

You'll notice as you read on that we have chosen to rate the Buy-ins and Antes on the low end of the financial scale. This is intentional. In order to win high-stakes Poker games like those described in later chapters where The Buy-in alone could reach $10,000.00, you first must prove yourself able to conquer those that begin with dimes and quarters.

DRAW AND STUD POKER

Purists will tell you that there are only two forms of 'real' Poker, Draw Poker and Stud Poker, truly because these are the basis from which all other competitive card games developed. Quite simply, Draw Poker is just that: players are entitled to draw cards from the Dealer after the initial cards are dealt. Players bet after receiving the initial cards, then discard and draw to replace the discards.

In Stud Poker, each Goddess plays with the initially dealt cards. Some cards are dealt face-down, some face-up, with betting taking place after each face-up card and the last face-down cards are dealt.

Draw Poker usually involves five cards, though Stud varies between five and seven. Each can be played one of two ways: high or low — or 'Lowball' as this method is commonly referred to, in which the lousiest Hand gets the pot's winnings!

In this chapter, we give each of these games and their many variations in-depth coverage. We are sure you will come to like certain games better than others, but also that you'll ultimately love and master them all, and in doing so, take those necessary first steps on your journey to becoming a true Poker Goddess.

So pull up a seat, pour the wine, and open that deck of cards. You're now going to play some Poker! Let the games begin!

5-Card Draw Poker

This is Poker at its simplest, the basic building block from which all other Poker relatives sprung. In standard variations of *5-Card Draw*, the Dealer can declare the addition of Wild Cards, though most purists balk and chose to play the game without them. That call belongs wholly with the Dealer, who may, as an example, include Jokers in the deck or call the one-eyed Jacks Wild.

As its name implies, this is a game where players are dealt five cards, and may discard some and draw others. It is best played by 3–6 Poker Goddesses.

THE BUY-IN:

Each Goddess antes a quarter into the Pot.

THE DEALER:

Deals five cards face-down around the table to each player.

PLAY:

Begins after players have assessed their cards and arranged them, organizing Pairs and High Cards together, and deciding which cards are to be discarded in the search to build a strong Poker Hand. Once Goddesses have evaluated their catch, they either fold (and are thus out of the game), or begin to bet. Betting starts with the Goddess at the Dealer's immediate left — if she folds, the next Goddess in line begins with a bet of ten cents. All players wanting to trade for new cards match the pot. It is now time to discard.

In standard Draw Poker, players are entitled to discard up to three cards. In one variation of **5-Card Draw**, a Goddess may discard four cards if she has caught an Ace, but she must turn that Ace up for all to see before receiving her new trade cards. The Dealer determines this option before play begins.

Players evaluate their catch cards, organize them into the highest and best Hand possible. Now that all players have their cards, another betting round commences, again beginning to the Dealer's left. Players either fold or bet, and one raising of the Bet is permitted ('I'll match your dime and raise you a dime.'). Once all Goddesses have declared their intentions, she who holds the Bid sets down her cards for all to see.

THE GOAL:

To win the Pot by showing the best Hand possible. You go, girl!

A CHIC SAMPLE HAND:

Poor Patsy has been dealt this deplorable Hand. What oh what can she do? Ditch all but your High Cards, honey! Ride that King/Ace combo in the hope of catching something to match. Even if you don't end up with a Pair or more after receiving your cards, in basic Draw Poker, a good High Hand can sometimes take the Pot!

STRATEGY:

The best advice for winning at *5-Card Draw* is to know the strength in your own Hand. If your initial deal cards are decent, bet on them and remain to see what you draw — you can always fold after that.

Catching a Pair on the initial deal is always a great beginning. Also, I have occasionally held onto a single High Card, such as an Ace or King, in the hope of catching another after the discard when new cards are dealt. My strategy on that involves the case of two players showing the same Pair during the showdown — she with the highest single card takes the Pot!

Rarely, I have seen a fellow Goddess catch a Flush or a Straight right on the initial deal! One always knows what is to follow when the Dealer asks, 'How many?' and she declares, 'None.' *Cue in the spooky music!*

While it isn't always easy to pick up the vibe from your fellow Poker Goddesses, after enough play, it is sometimes possible sometimes to get a feel for where your Hand ranks in comparison to theirs. It could be the quickness in which they bet, a facial expression, or their wild abandon-styled willingness to follow through to the end (this can also often-times work as one heck of a Bluff!).

Fold or bet on the strength of your own cards — it's as simple and pure as that!

7-Card Stud

7-Card Stud is to *5-Card Draw* what peanut butter is to jelly; what Ethel was to Lucy, a good cigar to a cold glass of dry champagne, a new credit card with an untapped limit to a day of crazed shopping. Not only do they compliment each other, they are linked by evolution, for these are Poker's Neanderthals, the early ancestors of the modern game we have all come to love and respect.

7-Card Stud is an easy-to-learn game that can be enjoyed by 3–7 Goddesses. It's dealt in a down-up manner: players receive two cards down, then a succession of four up, then the final one down, with rounds of betting in-between. Your goal is to make the best Poker Hand possible with the use of those seven cards.

This game also forms the basis for other games and variations — some of them absolutely wild and fabulous — dealt in a similar fashion, all of which will be covered later in the chapter.

THE BUY-IN:

Each Goddess antes a quarter into the Pot.

THE DEALER:

Deals two cards down around the table. Players look at those cards and assess them. Then the Dealer deals the next card up.

PLAY BEGINS:

After the first round of face-up cards are dealt. Betting begins with the Goddess who catches the Highest Card up. She pays a nickel into the Pot. All other players wanting to remain in the game match the Bet, and the Dealer continues, dealing another round up.

If a pair shows in the second round, the Bet automatically raises to a dime. High Hand showing always leads off the betting. Play continues in this manner for two more rounds, with betting at the end of each round, and players either fold or match the Bet. The seventh and last card is dealt down, and a showdown occurs, with the High Hand leading off the betting, usually a dime. The Pot can be raised once.

The Goddess with the High Hand wins and claims the Pot!

THE GOAL:

To best your fellow Goddesses and win the Pot.

A CHIC SAMPLE HAND:

Sue Ellen has been dealt this questionable mix of cards. What can she do? Since what you get is all you get with Stud Poker hands, she shall have to sink or swim based on this Hand. A savvy Sue Ellen will pay careful mind to the board and stick with her two Pairs only as long as she should. At the first sight of a Three of a Kind on the board, she'll have to fold 'em!

STRATEGY:

Unlike *5-Card Draw*, you have something of an advantage in this game by seeing more than half of your opponents' Hands. This should help you decide whether or not your own Hand stands up to scrutiny. The down side to this play of Poker is that there is no discard and draw to help augment your Hand. What you get dealt is it! But if you have good Hole Cards and feel confident you have the potential to win the Pot, stay in. If not, fold.

Variations of this game include the addition of Wild Cards, though again, most purists feel true *7-Card Stud* should be played without them. There are enough cousins of the game that do use Wild Cards, so you may want to follow their example. Master these first two original Poker games, and you have the basic building blocks for every other!

5-Card Stud

Ladies, when has even more stud ever been too much stud? The answer is never, hence the following variation. As its name implies, *5-Card Stud* is similar to its 7-Card sibling in that the method of play involves cards being dealt down, then up, and finally down.

This game is suited for 3-10 players and follows the same rules and strategies as *7-Card Stud* with minor differences.

THE BUY-IN:

Each player pays a quarter into the Pot.

THE DEALER:

Has the option of dealing cards in the following manner:

♣ Two cards down, three up
♦ One card down, four up
♥ One card down, three up, final card down

PLAY:

Commences after down cards and the first up card are dealt, with rounds of betting following each turn up of a card. The High Hand showing always starts bidding. A showdown round concludes the game, with the best Hand winning.

THE GOAL:

To make the best Poker Hand possible with your cards and win the Pot.

A CHIC SAMPLE HAND:

Miranda has been dealt this curious Hand. Like Sue Ellen, there will be no exchange of cards, so she must chose how best to utilize that which fate has dealt her. With a Pair showing, Miranda may wish to ride this one out and play with confidence, knowing that it may eventually intimidate her fellow Goddesses into folding!

STRATEGY:

As with *7-Card Stud*, players don't draw and discard cards, so if you're dealt garbage, there's no way to augment your Hand. A sound strategy is to watch the play on the table and assess your own Hand against what is showing, and remember, each time another player drops out, your chance of bluffing your way to a win betters. If you have cards up that appear intimidating but nothing to match them in the Hole, you may want to take a chance and ride it out to see if your fellow Goddesses blink and fold first.

While most Stud games don't involve deliciously handsome men in tear-away tuxedos that flash well-toned, oiled muscles as the name implies, they are fun nonetheless. But if your Poker parties are so well equipped, please do let me know. I'll be over to join you for cards!

Lowball

In this 'evil mirror universe' variation on *5-Card Draw,* players actually compete to get the worst Hand possible! That means forgetting the notion of drawing to catch Pairs, Straights or Flushes!

Lowball is best suited for 3–7 players, and while similar to *5-Card Draw,* the strategy for playing it is the exact opposite.

THE BUY-IN:

Each Goddess antes a quarter into the Pot.

THE DEALER:

Deals five cards down around the table to each player.

PLAY:

After cards are dealt, Goddesses arrange their Hands. The player to the left of the Dealer opens betting. All other players match or fold. Those who remain in the game purposefully discard any High Cards or Pairs in favor of the lowest ones. The Dealer then deals replacement cards, and a final round of betting takes place before the showdown.

THE GOAL:

To have the *worst* possible Hand, no Pairs, no High Cards. The Lowest Hand wins the Pot!

A CHIC SAMPLE HAND:

Edina has caught a Pair of Aces! But wait this is **Lowball**! Edina will wish to discard that Pair as well as the Jack in the hope of replacing them with the worst cards possible.

STRATEGY:

I've said it before and I'll say it again — fact *is* stranger than fiction!

Toss the Aces and Kings and keep the 2's and 3's — unless of course, you catch a Pair of them! If that is the case, you'll want to break up the Pair and hold on to the lowest, lousiest Hand imaginable. That's what wins a game of ***Lowball***!

Spit

Heavens! We all know that ladies don't spit — unless it has to do with this crazy little game, sometimes referred to as ***Spit in the Ocean***. ***Spit*** is another variation on ***5-Card Draw*** suitable for up to 7 players. And while there is no actual spitting, this wacky game does involve a wee bit of screaming.

In this version, each player receives four cards down. At any point during the deal, any Goddess can declare the magic word, '*Spit!*' in her most-spirited mezzo-soprano. The Dealer immediately flips up the next card in the deck face-up onto the table. This Community Card is Wild to everybody.

THE BUY-IN:

Each player antes a quarter into the Pot.

THE DEALER:

Deals four cards around, knowing that at any point, one of the Goddesses seated at the table will cry out, 'Spit.' The instant she does, the Community Spit Card is turned up and placed on the table. It is Wild to all players.

PLAY:

Play begins after all cards in the initial deal are dealt, and the Spit Card is declared. As an example, if the Spit Card is a 4, all 4 cards are Wild.

Players arrange their cards hoping to build the best Poker Hand possible. The Goddess to the Dealer's left opens the first round of betting, paying a dime into the Pot. All other players match the Bet or fold.

That done, players can discard up to three cards. The Dealer deals replacement cards, and players either fold or bet, with the Goddess to the Dealer's left kicking off the final round of betting. Players go to showdown and reveal their Hands. The High Hand wins the Pot!

THE GOAL:

To show the best Hand and claim the cash!

A CHIC SAMPLE HAND:

Annika has been dealt the following Hand. The Spit Wild Card is a 2. That means Annika holds a total of four 7's! She should discard the 8 and Ace, and draw two fresh cards in the hope of getting another.

STRATEGY:

Like other variants on *5-Card Draw*, this is an easy-to-learn and fun-to-play game. The same basic strategies apply: if your cards support the action, act! If they don't, then fold.

I have to admit, I've always liked this game, though I'm not sure why. Its name conjures crude images of nasty habits best left for men in locker rooms and bachelor parties, not a gathering of lovely ladies with far better manners! Still, there's something poetic about proving we can go round for round with the toughest of our male counterparts, and in that spirit, I encourage you to *Spit*.

Baseball

Though lacking the yummy tight pants and dimpled smiles of the fresh-faced men who play America's pastime, the game of ***Baseball*** is a neat variation on Poker suitable for 3-7 players. Seven cards are dealt in Stud-styled order: two down around to all players, then four up one round at a time, the last down. In ***Baseball***, recognized Poker Hands are sought. 3's and 9's are Wild, face up or dealt in the Hole. If a 3 is dealt face-up, that Goddess must match the Pot. A player dealt a 4 card up wins a free down card to help augment her Hand.

THE BUY-IN:

Each player antes a quarter into the Pot.

THE DEALER:

Deals two cards down around to each player. Players may look at their cards to assess them. The Dealer follows by dealing one card up around the table to each Goddess. Any player who catches a 4 card gets a free card down to augment their Hand. A 3 card dealt face-up is Wild, but she who catches it must match the Pot's total.

PLAY:

Once the first round of dealing is complete, the Goddess with the Highest Card on the table opens betting by paying a nickel into the Pot. Any 3 or 9 card dealt during the first round is considered the equivalent of an Ace and is thus the High Card showing unless a natural Ace is already present on the table. Once players have paid, the Dealer deals another card up to each player. If Wild Cards are showing in the first round to make a Pair on the board in the second, or if a natural Pair shows by the end of the second round, the Ante then doubles, increasing to a dime. Two more cards are dealt up and around in this manner, with the High Hand showing always leading the Bet (she who holds the High Hand will potentially change as play continues). The last card is dealt down.

By this point, some players may have folded. Those ladies still in the game, having assessed their Hands, will now face off in a showdown. The Goddess with the Highest Hand on the table leads the final betting, opening with a dime. Betting then continues to her left around the table, with players matching and possibly raising the Bet one time ('I'll match your quarter and raise you a quarter!').

The Goddess who makes the final Bet then declares her Hand, laying it down for all to see. Each remaining player in the game does similarly, and the player with the best Hand wins.

THE GOAL:

To show the best Hand possible and win the Pot.

A CHIC SAMPLE HAND:

Heroic Helena holds two Wild Cards in the illustration above. She also has three Spades, which gives her a nice Flush to ride with. But given the amount of Wild Cards still present at the table, she will have to monitor the game carefully.

STRATEGY:

As with all of the Stud-styled games, you'll have some insight into the potential of your own Hand by gauging it against those belonging to your fellow Goddesses. With so many Wild Cards — eight of them — and the potential for extra cards to augment your Hand, it's pretty safe to say if you ain't got 'em, fold 'em.

But if you have the cards to make a Royal Straight Flush or Four of a Kind, plant your feet firmly in the batter's box, knees slightly bent, choke up on that bat, and swing — you may just hit a home run!

Murder

Kindly put down that pearl-handled nail file! There will be no homicides in this game! Quite simply put, **Murder** is the game of **Baseball**, only down. In other words, all cards are dealt face-down and turned over in sequence, with each player hoping to best the Hand that's come before hers.

Murder is not dealt Stud-style; ALL cards are dealt down. As in **Baseball**, recognized Poker Hands are sought. 3's and 9's are Wild. If any player turns up a 4 card, she automatically wins a free card to help augment her Hand.

THE BUY-IN:

Each player antes a quarter into the Pot.

THE DEALER:

Then deals seven cards down around to each player. Players may not look at their cards yet.

PLAY:

Once cards have been dealt, the Goddess to the Dealer's left begins play, flipping her top card up for all to see. No matter what she flips up, she now has the Highest Hand on the table and for the moment, goes no further in revealing her cards. Doesn't matter if she turns up a 2 card, or an Ace — she's temporarily the reigning Diva! With that 2 or Ace, she then bids a nickel to the Pot. All other players will want to match the Bid at this point and remain in the game, as they have yet to see their cards!

The next Goddess then flips her top card. If the first player has a 2 showing, she must beat it. Any card higher than the 2 beats her, so if a 5 shows, the second Goddess ceases flipping. Another nickel is added to the Pot. If the first Goddess flips an Ace card, and the second flips an Ace then a 6, she's beaten the first Ace Hand with Ace-6.

The third player must then beat the second Goddess' Hand, and will flip until she does just that. She may flip up four cards to get there before unearthing, say, a Pair of 10s. Once a Pair is reached, the Bet is automatically raised from a nickel to a dime.

The next player in line must then beat her predecessor's Pair of 10's. With the addition of the 3 and 9 Wild Cards, great Hands can quickly build! And again, each time a player turns up a 4, she is dealt an extra card down to help augment her Hand.

Once play swings back to the original Goddess who flipped the single card to kick off the game, she must beat the Highest Hand revealed to that point. Play continues in this manner around the table, with the Pot building and some Goddesses folding after turning up the last of their cards.

THE GOAL:

To 'murder' your fellow Poker players by turning up the best Hand on the table, thus winning what can amount to be a significant Pot.

A CHIC SAMPLE HAND:

Intrepid Kate has caught this mediocre **Murder** Hand. The free card for her 4 isn't much help. Kate must dig in her boot heels and boldly face her adversaries on a trio of Jacks. A smart woman, she will watch the play around the table and bet only as far as the strength of her own Hands permits.

STRATEGY:

There's an added randomness to **Murder** not found in most other Poker games in that you don't get to see your cards before everybody else does! So in effect with this one, it's not always how well you play to win, but how willing you are to lose, something your savvy fellow Goddesses may count on as more and more cards are turned up.

It is not uncommon to see Straight Flushes, Royal Flushes, Four of a Kind or even Five of a Kind given the number of Wild Cards in this game. So if you've turned up four of your seven down cards and caught nothing, it's a pretty good bet that it's time to accept defeat. But if you've taken time to notice what is showing on the table, and you have the makings of a good suit — a Wild Card, some Face cards, or the basis for a Flush or Straight — there's a good chance you may want to ride it out until the end to see the last of those hidden cards.

I've seen an elderly friend go to the last card every time when playing this game, even when she's had nothing on the table worth hoping for! She just can't stand the idea of letting even one of those cards go unseen. But as with all of the games described in this book, the more one plays **Murder**, the more you'll acquire a feel for the length you're willing to go. All the wishful thinking in the world won't boost a

crummy Hand. If you get the goods, let it ride. If not, murder that Hand! Just make sure to leave the jeweled daggers
and pearl-handled lady's pistols in your purses!

Football

Football is another of **Baseball**'s siblings. I'm not sure why this variation was named thus, as it lacks cheerleaders, pigskin, and any
form of tackling. As with **Baseball**, **Football** is dealt with the first
two cards down, the next four up, and the last down, but with one
marked difference. In **Football**, 4's and 6's are Wild. When a 4 card
turns up, the Goddess bequeathed with it must then match the Pot
or drop out of the game. A deuce dealt up entitles that player to an
extra Hole Card. Deuces in the Hole are not Wild.

THE BUY-IN:

Players each ante a quarter into the Pot.

THE DEALER:

Deals two cards down to each Goddess. Once players have
assessed their down cards, the Dealer deals one card up. The
player with the Highest Card showing kicks off the betting,
paying a nickel to the Pot. Each player interested in continuing
the game matches the nickel Bet. If a Wild Card shows on the
table, betting on the next Hand automatically raises to a dime,
as the next round of cards dealt face-up will result in a Pair.

PLAY:

Play continues in this manner, with four cards total dealt up, and the last two dealt down. Once the Dealer has slipped each Goddess her seventh and final Hole Card, players assess their Hands. Standard Poker Hands apply.

She who has the Highest Hand showing opens the final betting by paying a dime into the Pot. The player to her right then has the option of raising the Bet after everybody who wishes to compete for the Pot has matched it. Once the Bet is matched and all have declared their intentions, players show their Hands.

THE GOAL:

To show the best Hand at the end of the deal and win the Pot.

A CHIC SAMPLE HAND:

Maya has caught the following cards. Her best bet in this Hand is to take her 9 of Clubs, 10 of Diamonds, and Jack of Diamonds and pair them up with the two Wild Cards (the second thanks to her 2 card catch in the initial deal). This will give her a 9, 10, J, Q, K-high Straight.

STRATEGY:

As with *Baseball*, in order to win the game of *Football*, a player must be aware of what is showing on the table and feel confident that her own Hand is strong enough to beat it. Only you can see your Hole Cards, and if they happen to support what you've got showing up on the table, it's probably worth taking a chance to force your opponents to divulge their Hands before folding.

You don't need Astroturf, shoulder pads, helmets, and a quarterback to play this one. You just have to show up with a winning attitude, ready to do battle against your opponents. Spiked shoes, optional.

Chicago

Like Los Angeles, New York, Boston, and Seattle, Chicago has, Hands down, one of the coolest literary scenes on the planet. Home to poets, writers, and all sorts of hip artist types, it also has the notorious distinction of being this Poker variation's namesake.

Chicago is dealt Stud-styled, like *Football*, though the similarities end there. A Pair of Jacks or better is required to open the game for final betting. Aces in the hole are Wild. A high Spade card down splits the Pot with the winner. Seems pretty clear and simple, you say? Well, after a disastrous long-distance love affair, I know firsthand just what a heartbreaker the Windy City can be!

Right when you think you've got an excellent Hand showing, a high Spade or an Ace in the Hole, the whole thing can come to a crashing halt with the appearance of one card, that cruel witch, the Queen of Spades...

THE BUY-IN:

Each player pays a quarter into the Pot.

THE DEALER:

Deals two cards down to each player, then one up.

PLAY:

In *Chicago*, your aim is to build the best Poker Hand possible using your down cards and those turned up on the board. Play begins after Goddesses have had a chance to assess their cards. The player with the Highest Hand showing on the table leads off the betting, paying a nickel into the Pot. Other Goddesses match the Pot, and a second round of cards is dealt around the table.

If a Pair shows after this second round, the Bet increases to a dime. Play continues in this manner for a third and fourth round, with betting at each conclusion. After the fourth round, unless a Pair of Jacks or better is showing up on the table, the round dies — there must be a Pair of Jacks or better to open the showdown. If not, cards are shuffled and the deal passes to the original Dealer's left. Each time a round ends without being opened, players must pay the original bet of twenty-five cents into the Pot.

Chicago continues in this manner, round after round until a natural Pair of Jacks or better shows. And to make matters more complex, sometimes, just when you achieve that, seemingly out of nowhere that darn desPot, the Queen of Spades, appears! One glance from her cold and beady eyes brings the game to a crashing halt. You could have two Ace cards in the Hole and a Pair of Jacks showing! She doesn't care. She's just put a hex on the round. When the Queen of Spades rears her pinched face, all cards get automatically tossed away. The round dies, and the deal passes to the next Goddess in line from the left. Players pay again, the cards are reshuffled, and then re-dealt.

Eventually, the Poker Gods will shine down upon you, and that elusive Pair of Jacks or better will show, the Queen will have retired to her throne room, and the High Hand showing will begin a round of showdown betting. The best Poker Hand wins, and remember, she who holds the highest Spade card DOWN splits the Pot!

THE GOAL:

To win big in the Windy City by holding either the best Poker Hand or the high Spade card down, which splits the Pot.

A CHIC SAMPLE HAND:

Alexis has caught this terrible Hand while wheeling and dealing in *Chicago.* She doesn't have the required Pair of Jacks or better to open; however, archrival Crystal does. Should Alexis fold and walk away? Absolutely not! Before grabbing a Handful of Crystal's golden hair or pushing her into the nearest duck pond, Alexis will instead wish to remain in the game. Remember — a HIGH SPADE DOWN splits the Pot with the winner, and she's got that 10 card to her credit!

STRATEGY:

You may find *Chicago* to be your kind'a town! It certainly is a challenging take on *7-Card Stud* that can continue on for many rounds until the right combination of cards presents itself. Thus, it's usually a good bet to get to this one fairly early in your Poker night festivities, as it has a tendency to eat up a lot of time.

Many new players to *Chicago* mistakenly forget that all Aces are not Wild. Only Ace cards dealt down are Wild Cards. Any turned up on the board can only help you as High Cards in your Poker Hand.

While similar strategies for winning at Stud Poker apply to *Chicago*, there are certain differences. For instance, the Queen of Spades death card has the Potential to throw a monkey wrench into any plans you may have — unless you have Her Majesty secretly tucked safely in the Hole, at which point she can become a great ally even if you have garbage to bet on, and somebody else shows the right cards to open.

It's rarely a good idea to fold in *Chicago*. Fold in the first round and you are out of a game that can go for many rounds! There will be numerous opportunities to win the Pot — or at least part of it should you have a high Spade down and the showdown betting becomes open. Because of its nature, the Pot in *Chicago* tends to swell quickly.

Obviously, the best Hand to catch is one where you have not only the High Hand, but also the high Spade — the Ace — in the Hole! I've seen this happen and have won *Chicago* many times this way myself. A good bit of strategy is to stick it out, and always stay in the game once the Bet is opened if you have even a lowly Spade card down. If nobody else stays in with a Spade, you can take half that Pot on a crummy Spade card alone!

Unlike the city it was named after which I always enjoy visiting, *Chicago* is not my favorite variant on *7-Card Stud*. But I certainly enjoy it in metered doses. The problem is, once the Dealer declares we're all about to take a trip on the Elevated Train to the Loop for a night in the Windy City, the doses are more like *over*-doses. *Chicago* plods on. And on. And on.

This one may just leave you humming Frank Sinatra's rendition of 'Chicago' over and over again ad nauseum.

Jacks Are Better — Progressive

Jacks Are Better — Progressive, like its close cousin *Chicago*, is a game that often requires multiple rounds of play in order to open the Pot up to showdown betting. Ideal for 3-6 gal-pals, *Jacks Are Better* is dealt Stud-styled with two cards down, four up, and two down, but with a unique twist: a Pair of Jacks or better is required to open the bidding. If that fails to happen in the first round, cards are re-dealt and now a Pair of Queens is the minimum required Hand to open the round to showdown betting.

The minimum required Hand progresses up to a Pair of Kings, then a Pair of Aces, then back down to Kings, Queens, and Jacks — and then up again if that minimum required Hand to open doesn't present itself up.

THE BUY-IN:

Each Goddess pays a quarter into the Pot.

THE DEALER:

Deals two cards down around the table to each player.

PLAY:

Once Goddesses have had a chance to assess their cards, the Dealer deals one card up to each player. Betting begins with the Goddess who catches the highest card up. She pays a nickel into the Pot. All other players match the Bet, and the Dealer continues, dealing another round up.

If a Pair shows in the second round, the Bet automatically raises to a dime. High Hand showing always leads off the betting. Play continues in this manner for a third round with betting, but if at the end of the fourth round of cards dealt up a Pair of Jacks or better isn't caught, the round officially ends. Players board their cards and pay another quarter into the Pot.

The deal passes to the left of the original dealer, cards are reshuffled, and re-dealt. Now, things have progressed to a Pair of Queens. The entire process from the first round is replayed exactly, right to that fourth card flipped up. If a Pair of Queens fails to manifest during the round, cards are discarded, another twenty-five cents is paid into the Pot, and the minimum required Hand becomes a Pair of Kings.

Should play reach a Pair of Aces and that minimum required Hand not be met, the next round progresses back to a Pair of Kings. A Pair of Queens follows, then a Pair of Jacks, backwards and forwards in order until the required Pair is turned up.

Once the required Pair manifests, players receive their

seventh card, down. The required Pair opens the betting, and players either bet or fold, hoping to flash the Highest Hand and win what can amount to quite a substantial Poker Pot.

THE GOAL:

To have the Poker Hand that wins the Pot.

A CHIC SAMPLE HAND:

Olivia has caught this Hand, which is strong enough to open the round of betting. Lovely Livvie will want to toss the 2 and 4, keep her Pair of Jacks and the Ace as well in the hope of drawing another Ace to match.

STRATEGY:

Play this one the way you would any Stud-style Poker game, knowing that the likelihood of multiple rounds exists. It's rare that *Jacks Are Better* concludes quickly. In most cases, the game spirals forward and down the Progressive scale, and often times maddeningly so! Isn't it always the way that when the minimum required Hand is a Pair of Queens, you get dealt a Pair of Jacks up — a round late and a Face Card short!

Remember, it doesn't matter what you have down initially. If nobody opens with that minimum required Pair, the round will end. Another faulty assumption is that the opening Hand also happens to be the highest on the table. It may not be! It may simply be the Highest Hand showing.

Pots in *Jacks Are Better* have a tendency to rise quickly, meaning if you are going to buy-in to play it, you should ride it through to the end, not folding your cards in early rounds if the minimum required Pair doesn't show.

Like *Chicago*, this one can go on for a while. I'm convinced that somewhere out there, trapped in a warp in the time-space continuum, there's a group of women who innocently began a game of *Jacks Are Better — Progressive* and are still playing it, oblivious to the passing of years, shuffling and re-dealing the cards for this one, up and down, again and again, as they search for that minimum Pair!

Anaconda

What a wild and strange game this is, this sneaky little snake called *Anaconda*! Also known to some enthusiasts as *Pass the Trash*, *Anaconda* is a passing game suited for 4-7 of your friends. In it, you shuttle off part of your Hand to the player to your left, and receive cards from the Goddess at your right en route to making either the best or worst Poker Hand possible. Like having a high Spade down in *Chicago*, the winnings in *Anaconda* are split high/low between the best Hand and the worst, and the path to determining which route you will go is likely to be decided by the cards tossed your way.

I resisted playing this game at first. With its element of card passing, it felt too deceptive and anarchist to me. Additionally, I couldn't get past the name — I always believed Eve got a bum rap thanks to that damn snake way back when in the Garden of Eden. But like Eve and the apple, I ultimately gave in to temptation, and played several games of *Anaconda* with the ladies. Since then, I can honestly relate to why she did it!

THE BUY-IN:

Starts with each player paying a quarter into the Pot. All further betting commences after cards are passed, so read on, my lovelies!

THE DEALER:

Deals seven cards down to each player. Players assess their cards and decide, based upon their catch, which to pass.

PLAY:

Anaconda begins with each player selecting three cards to discard face-down to the Goddess at her left. Players then take those three pass cards and arrange them in their Hands, assess them, and a round of betting begins at the Dealer's left, usually a dime. Players match the Pot.

After picking up the three cards from the player to the right, each Goddess then passes two more cards to the left. Another round of betting kicks off. A final pass then takes place, this time with a single card. A final dime Bet is made, after which each player discards two cards into the center of the table as true discards, leaving all with five remaining in their Hand.

Each Goddess assesses her Hand, then lines all five cards face-down on the table in the order she wishes to expose them to the rest of the players at the table. The Dealer then takes charge, telling every player to 'Flip!' Players reveal one card in their Hand, turning it up for all to see.

Seeing these Flip Cards, a round of betting commences to the Dealer's left. All players match the bet. The Dealer again declares, 'Flip!' At that cue, players turn over a second card. Another round of betting commences. Play continues in this manner, with players revealing a third and fourth card, with betting at each conclusion. A final round of betting commences around the table in anticipation of the showdown, when players turn over their fifth card. Highest Hand wins the Pot, splitting it with the lowest.

THE GOAL:

To be she who holds either the best or worst Poker Hand.

A CHIC SAMPLE HAND:

Red Alert! Roxann has named 3's and 5's Wild, and for that, Jeri has one bodacious Hand! As it stands, she has a four-Ace catch. Since she will have to 'pass the trash', that means discarding anything that isn't an Ace or a Wild Card. However, Roxann may wish to take an alternate approach. Since the Lowball Hand splits the Pot, she could possibly do away with all of her good cards, though her best bet will likely be to stick with the treasure and hope that somebody passes her one more good card in their search for trash.

STRATEGY:

Though fairly new to the game of *Anaconda*, I've noticed that most players routinely aim for high Poker Hands, and as thus hold onto good High Cards. Sensing this, at one point, I intentionally changed my strategy and aimed for the Lowball Hand. I ended up getting half of a fairly substantial Pot.

During the Flip Stage, bluffing can play an integral part of winning the game should you opt for the Lowball approach. If you have what looks to be a Straight or a Flush, for example showing a 5, 6, 7, 8 in different suits or four cards all in the same, you may just bluff the rest of your fellow players into folding before the final round of betting. Imagine their surprise when you turn over a card that doesn't match the rest! In this strategy, the Low Hand doesn't just split the Pot; it takes everything!

Variations on *Anaconda* include the addition of Wild Cards, which can quickly turn the game into a high-hand free-for-all. Few players are going to part with Wild Cards during the three passing rounds anymore than they would a Pair of Aces. If you catch good High Cards, work for that High Hand. But if you're getting garbage, try going in the opposite direction: aim low, win big!

Follow the Queen

This one's a stinker! Suitable for 3–7 Goddesses, it is played Stud-style, with cards dealt two face-down followed by four face-up and the last card down. There's one marked difference in **Follow the Queen**: the relevance of the Queen card. Queens in the Hole are Wild. Each time a Queen turns up on the table, the card that immediately follows becomes Wild to all players. But just when you think you've got a killer Hand because the card turned up following the Queen is a 5 and your Hand is loaded with 5 cards — another Queen is turned up, and with it, a different Wild Card follows, effectively canceling out your Four of a Kind.

This baby is sometimes referred to simply as **Queens**, and due to the very nature just mentioned, it may leave you searching for the nearest guillotine and shouting, 'Off with her head!'

THE BUY-IN:

Each player antes a quarter into the Pot.

THE DEALER:

Deals two cards down to each Goddess. Players assess their Hole Cards. Dealer then deals one card up to each player.

PLAY:

Begins with a round of betting after the first face-up cards are dealt. The High Card on the table kicks off the bidding — if there are four of you, and one has a 6, one has a 7, one a Jack, and one a King, she holding the King card opens, paying a nickel into the Pot. The Dealer then deals a second round of cards up.

If a Queen card is revealed, the Dealer flips the very next card up and sets it centrally on the table. That card is an additional Wild Card to everybody and automatically increases the betting from a nickel to a dime, since each player now has a Pair showing on the table. If the follow card is a Jack, now every Jack in your Hand is Wild whether it is up or down. High Hand again bets, and all Goddesses must match or fold.

A third card is dealt around face-up to each Goddess. Remember that lady holding all the Jacks in her Hand? If another Queen card is flipped in this round, a new Wild Card will be turned up. Suddenly, those Jacks aren't all that anymore! A new Wild Card replaces Jacks. Say the card is a 4. Now, up or down, all 4 cards are Wild. High Hand again leads the betting.

Play continues for a fourth round in this manner, with betting at the end. By this point, the Community Wild Cards, if any, have been established. Remember — there's no guarantee that a Queen is going to surface! At the end of the fourth round, the Dealer deals the final card down. Each Goddess assesses her Hand, deciding whether to remain in the game or fold.

Once that has been decided, the Highest Hand showing leads off a final betting round. Goddesses go head to head for the showdown, with the best Poker Hand winning.

THE GOAL:

To be crowned Her Royal Majesty in the game of *Follow the Queen* by showing the top Hand that wins the Pot!

A CHIC SAMPLE HAND:

Saffron has been dealt the following Hand. At the very least, she has three Kings, thanks to her Queen in the Hole. But if a Queen is turned up elsewhere on the table, her Hand will improve. She may be able to stretch her Three of a Kind into a Four of a Kind; or create a Royal Straight Flush using her Ace and King of Spades. Of course, given the nature of **Queens**, this might be all Saffron gets.

STRATEGY:

Be prepared for a great deal of griping to accompany the shift in Wild Cards, but to quote, *let them eat cake!*

Having a great group of Wild Cards and the prospect of losing them to the random flip of a Queen card will likely keep you and your fellow maidens on the edge of your thrones at the Poker table! The charm of ***Follow the Queen*** — that random element which can change allegiances in the blink of an eye — is also cause to both love and hate this game.

The Potential of catching so many Wild Cards makes ***Follow the Queen*** worth riding all the way to the end. Just don't get too comfortable with them until all cards are turned up. Remember that only Queens in the Hole are Wild — unless, of course, the Dealer flips a Queen and follows by turning up another Queen, which sometimes happens! Play this one as you would any other Poker game, with attention to making the best Hand possible. And if you do indeed have cake, make sure that it's chocolate and pass me a slice!

Salt & Pepper

Salt & Pepper is a Wild Card bonanza that can be played as a *5-Card Draw* game, or *7-Card Stud*-styled, down. When played down like *Baseball* or *Follow the Queen*, *Salt & Pepper* boasts its own similar brand of rules. When played up draw-style, players discard and draw in the hope of getting the best Hand possible.

Without adieu, toss a pinch of salt over your shoulder for luck and let's add some seasoning to what promises to be a scrumptious banquet!

Salt & Pepper (5-Card Draw)

Best suited for 3–7 Goddesses, this one follows the same basic format as other Draw Poker games.

THE BUY-IN:

Each player antes a quarter into the Pot.

THE DEALER:

Deals five cards around to each player.

PLAY:

Begins after all Goddesses assess their Hands. In both up

and down variations of **Salt & Pepper**, each of the following cards are Wild:

♣ 2's
♦ 4's
♥ 10's
♠ One-eyed Jacks

Players strive to make the best Poker Hand possible. The Goddess to the Dealer's left opens the first round of betting with a nickel. All players match the Bet and discard. The Dealer deals replacement cards.

Once players have had a chance to assess their catches, the Goddess to the Dealer's left opens the final round of bidding with a dime. Players either fold or match the Pot. Once everybody has declared their intentions, players reveal their cards. The Highest Hand wins the Pot.

GOAL:

To show the best Poker Hand and win the Pot.

A CHIC SAMPLE HAND:

Slinky Samantha has been dealt this tempting quintet of cards — an Ace and two Wild Cards. She should dump the

3 of Hearts and 9 of Spades and play for something to match.

STRATEGY:

In the Wild Card bonanza, *Salt & Pepper*, it's pretty easy to build one heck of a Poker Hand. It is not uncommon to see Five of a Kind and Royal Flushes, especially in the Stud-styled version where players hold 7 cards.

Should your Hand lack a healthy combination of 2's, 4's, 10's, or a one-eyed Jack, fold. If you get good cards, ride the Hand out.

Salt & Pepper (7-Card Stud)

Best suited for 3–6 Goddesses, play this as you would any Stud-styled game, with attention to the Wild Cards: 2's, 4's, 10's, and one-eyed Jacks.

THE BUY-IN:

Players pay a quarter into the Pot.

THE DEALER:

Deals two cards down, then one up.

PLAY:

Goddesses assess their Hole Cards. The player with the Highest Card showing on the table opens the betting and pays a nickel into the Pot. If more than one Goddess has been dealt a Wild Card — the equivalent of an Ace — the player closest to the Dealer's left opens bidding. A natural Ace supercedes any Wild Cards when it comes to opening the Bid; in other words, if there are two Wild Cards and an Ace on the table, the holder of the Ace opens betting. If two Aces are present, the Goddess closest to the Dealer's left opens.

Once everyone has paid into the Pot, the Dealer deals a second round of cards up to each Goddess. Another round of betting ensues, with the Highest Hand leading off. If a Pair shows, the betting raises automatically to a dime. Two more rounds of identical play follow, with the seventh card dealt down.

The Highest Hand leads off the showdown betting. Goddesses either match or fold, and when all have declared, players show their cards. The best Poker Hand wins!

THE GOAL:

To have the best Poker Hand on the table and win the Pot.

A CHIC SAMPLE HAND:

Kira has flipped up, in sequence, the following cards. At best, she shows a Diamond Flush. Kira will fold if one of her fellow Goddesses flips something better.

STRATEGY:

Play Stud-styled *Salt & Pepper* as you would similar games, but with attention to one glaring detail: the amount of Potential Wild Cards. If you see your fellow players catching 2's, 4's, and 10's with ease and you're holding nothing three rounds into play, err on the side of sanity and humility, and fold.

Yet another variation on *Salt & Pepper* involves dealing all 7 cards down and playing it much like you would the game of *Murder*, only with its myriad of Wild Cards as opposed to 3's and 9's. No matter how you play *Salt & Pepper*, this is a great one to master. It's easy, quick, and seasoned to taste!

Texas Hold 'em

Yeehaw!

As legends go, they grow things big in Texas, and this yellow rose sibling of traditional Poker is no exception. **Texas Hold 'em** has become one of the darlings of the professional Poker circuit for its ability to quickly build a Pot to monumental proportions. It is also the game of choice at Binion's Horseshoe Casino's famous high-stakes World Series of Poker.

This is a layered game that involves Blind Bets, bluffing, and the sharing of Community Cards. It is best suited for up to nine of your fellow Southern Belles. Players are only dealt two Hole Cards down, with three cards up to the table, then an additional sixth and seventh up after with rounds of betting in between. The goal is to make the best five-card Hand from these seven cards.

The discerning Goddess will soon realize the intricate nature of this beast, and that gaining a sense of the subtle differences between her Hand and her opponents' Hands is the key to victory when visiting the Lone Star State.

THE BUY-IN:

Each Goddess pays a quarter into the Pot. The Dealer sets a low and high betting limit for two rounds of 'Blind' betting that occur after the cards have been dealt (you'll see how quickly the Pot in this one rises, so get that bankroll ready, Cowgirls!).

THE DEALER:

Deals two cards down to each player. Goddesses are not allowed to look at these cards until a round of Blind betting begins.

PLAY:

A Blind Bet is one that occurs before players are entitled a peek at their cards. The first Bet, called the 'Small Blind,' automatically occurs to the Dealer's immediate left. The Goddess seated in the Small Blind seat pays a percentage of the Pot's total — either a quarter of the total or half, based on the Dealer's say-so (if you have two bucks in the Pot, she generally pays either fifty cents or a dollar). The next Blind Bet, referred to as the 'Big Blind' occurs to the Goddess seated next in line, two seats to the left of the Dealer. She must kick in the full value of the minimum Bet established by the Dealer — if your Pot is two dollars, the minimum Bid is usually half that. Again, players either match the Bet or fold.

Once the Blinds have been made, each Goddess is entitled to look at her Hole Cards.

The Dealer then deals three cards face-up into the center of the table. These are called the 'Flop Cards' and are Community to everybody. A round of betting begins after the Flop Cards are dealt, beginning to the Goddess at the Dealer's left at the Small Blind seat (unlike the Blind Bets, these can be at a smaller set limit, say a quarter). After that, another card is dealt face-up. This card is known as the 'Turn.' Another round of betting ensues, again starting at the Small Blind seat. The betting in this round generally raises back to the high end of the Dealer's set limit, and that Bet can be raised once it has passed around the table. A fifth Community Card called the 'River' completes the Community Cards. Another round of betting (usually equal to the Turn limits) follows.

Using their two Hole Cards and the Community Cards, each Goddess strives to make the best five-card Poker Hand possible. After the River Card round concludes, players go to showdown, with betting beginning to the left of the Dealer. Goddesses either bet or fold, and once all have declared their intentions, players reveal their Hands. The Belle with the best cleans up what usually ends up amounting to a substantial Pot!

THE GOAL:

To be the best in the West! The Highest Hand — or the last Goddess standing — cleans up!

A CHIC SAMPLE HAND:

Sammy Joe sashays up to the *Texas Hold 'em* table and catches the following. She holds two Pairs — Aces and 9's — — and may wish to see this Hand through to its finale.

STRATEGY:

Given the nature of Pots to swell quickly in *Texas Hold 'em*, the best strategy for winning this game is to either trust your Hand or fold it. If you have something worth going all the way on, stay in. If not, know when to fold 'em!

My fellow Goddesses and I haven't played this one much despite its larger-than-life reputation. After a particularly harrowing nine months spent living in Texas, I have personally tended to shy away from it. This may be an unfair assessment, as I love Poker in all its many guises, but it is an honest one.

When we have indulged in *Texas Hold 'em*, I've remained in the game holding a bare Ace in the Hole Cards and somehow walked away with the Pot, matching it to a King on the Community Cards for a paltry High Card win. I based my strategy entirely on the betting play of my fellow Goddesses who caught less and were noticeably aghast by the obvious anemia of the Community Cards. In other instances, I've seen a High Pair or Three of a Kind clean up when I was dealt a Low Pair down.

Note: *Omaha* is a popular variation on the game of *Texas Hold 'em* in which players are dealt four cards down as opposed to two, though Goddesses must still make the best five-card Poker Hand using two down cards and three from the table.

52

Without compare, this is my absolute favorite Poker game. The purists and Poker Gods alike may burn my shapely maiden-form in effigy for admitting this, but *feh*, I say — I love **52**!

This game is often crudely referred to as **Balls** or **Guts**, theoretically due to the amount of gumption required to play it and the resolve to follow it through to its climactic ending. **52** is an insane variation on **5-Card Draw** that utilizes three clusters of Wild Cards. Players aim to build the best Poker Hands possible (a fairly easy task given the amount of Potential Wild Cards!). But along with this Bacchanalian madness comes an element of great risk: any player who stays in this game and loses the round has to match the Pot! That means the Pot swells larger and larger, as does your payoff into it if you fail to beat your opponents!

To ensure fairness, **52** also employs an interesting device — the use of a coin to declare a player's intention to remain in the Hand or to fold.

THE BUY-IN:

Each player pays a quarter into the Pot.

THE DEALER:

Declares three individual cards as being Wild and deals five cards around the table. Some of our favorite and more famous/infamous Wild Card combinations are:

♣ 3's, 5's, 7's
♦ 2's, 4's, 10's
♥ Aces, Kings, 8's
♠ 4's, 6's, 8's
♣ 2's, 3's, 4's,
♦ 5's, 7's, 9's
♥ Jacks, Queens, Kings
♠ 10's, Jacks, Queens
♣ 3's, 7's, Jacks
♦ No Wild Cards

Or the ultimate combination...

♥ 5's, 9's, Queens

Note: With this varied and expansive roster of Wild Cards, it is sometimes prudent to jot them down on a piece of paper for the duration of the game should confusion arise.

PLAY:

Begins after players have evaluated their cards. Each Goddess discards and draws up to 3 replacement cards. The declared Wild Cards are Wild to everybody. If the Dealer says 5's, 9's, and Queens are Wild, *every* 5, 9, and Queen card is your friend!

Once players decide upon their Hands, each Goddess places a coin on the table directly in front of it. Shielding from the eyes of others with one Hand, she turns it to heads or tails with the other and clasps it under her palm. This is to aid her in declaring her intentions: showing *heads* up means she intends to draw cards and stay in the round. *Tails* is an indication that she plans to fold for the round (folding from any round of 52 does not affect players joining the next round and remaining in the game).

The Dealer then calls for players to show their coins. Any Goddess flashing tails sits back and watches the showdown that follows, courtesy of those who stayed in by showing heads. The showdown commences, with players revealing their cards. The player with the best Poker Hand wins and takes the Pot. But anybody who remained for the showdown must now match the Pot's total.

If six of you seated around the card table pay into the Pot, that's $1.50. Should two of you drop and four of you stay in the round, the three who lose must match that buck-fifty, meaning the Pot swells to $4.50.

Once the Pot is matched, the deal passes to the Goddess seated at the original dealer's left. She shuffles and deals five new cards for the next round of play. The Wild Cards remain the same so long as there is money in the Pot and cannot be changed until the Pot is emptied. Play continues in the same manner as the first round, but now there is $4.50 at stake to win — or lose if you stay in the game and are bested by a player with a better Hand!

52 only ends when the Pot has grown to a point that scares all but one player from staying in the round. When

only one coin shows heads, the game ends, and the holder of that coin takes all.

THE GOAL:

To build the best Poker Hands round to round, and to win what can amount to a very substantial Pot.

A CHIC SAMPLE HAND:

Hoshi has caught this Hand. Jolene has named 5's, 9's, and Queens Wild, bless her heart! Enterprising Hoshi will want to dump the 2 of Spades and Jack of Diamonds and draw two cards in search of another Ace or something Wild, and given the bevy of Wild Cards in 52, she just may get it!

STRATEGY:

Perhaps in no other game does a player's savvy come into call as in 52. Given the plethora of Wild Cards, it isn't uncommon to see Five of a Kind and Royal Flush Hands competing around the table. If you don't have similar cards to support meeting your fellow Goddesses head-on, turn that coin to tails and wait for the next round to begin.

Early on, my card playing pals and I established a ceiling limit on 52. Once the Pot reaches $5.00, it goes no higher.

This means that for the last Hand after the limit is reached, every player remains in, and she holding the best Hand wins the Pot. The game ends without the Pot being paid into further. If not for this mechanism, **52** could have you signing unbelievable IOU's and mortgaging the house!

This is such a fun and exciting game, it remains a classic in our friendly circle. Play it smart and keep it sane and you may find it similarly received in yours!

Criss-Cross

This is a creative little variation on standard Poker that I haven't appreciated much until lately, due entirely to the fact I've somehow never been very good at it! Is this a reflection on the player or the game — you will have to decide for yourself!

In *Criss-Cross*, each Goddess is dealt only two cards. Five cards are dealt into the center of the table in the pattern of a cross, three horizontally, then one up and one below the center card to make a vertical bar. Using their two cards, players try to make the best five-card Hand by betting on ONE bar of three cards in the cross (you can't use all five cards, only three running in one direction to augment your initial deal cards).

THE BUY-IN:

Each player ponies a quarter into the Pot.

THE DEALER:

Deals two cards face-down to each player, then five cards down at the center of the table, forming a cross in the following manner:

CARD

CARD   CARD   CARD

CARD

PLAY:

Begins with the dealer turning over each of the five Criss-Cross Cards, one at a time. After each card is revealed, a round of betting kicks off, beginning at the Dealer's left. Betting on the first three cards is a nickel. For the final two cards, the Bet raises to a dime. The Dealer decides which three cards are to be revealed first, and which two will be shown last.

After the last card is revealed and the final dime is paid into the Pot, players will go head to head in a showdown. The player to the Dealer's left leads off the bidding, and using one bar of cards running in one direction, three up and down, or three across, each Goddess makes the best Poker Hand possible. She who does, wins!

THE GOAL:

To make the best Hand possible, and win the Pot.

A CHIC SAMPLE HAND:

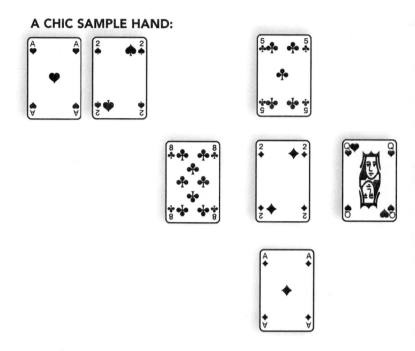

Marina holds an Ace of Hearts and a 2 of Spades in her Hand. By matching the up-and-down direction of the Criss-Cross, she can make two Pairs: Aces and 2's.

STRATEGY:

One of the reasons I think I've been slow to warm up to **Criss-Cross** is its random and chaotic nature. Whatever you're dealt down is it — you can't draw new cards, and you're at the mercy of the ones in the cross, so if you get garbage you're stuck with it.

My turnaround in liking this game came about after a verbal drumming by my fabulous writing partner, who very clearly reminded me of the creative nature of this Poker beast. It is a neat and different variation to the staid approach to Poker, and that alone endeared it to me.

Simply, if your cards don't support staying in, fold. If you are a curious creature, as I am, put up your nickels and dimes to see if something is lurking in that cross pattern that will actually help you create a decent Poker Hand. Since gaining a new-found affinity for **Criss-Cross**, I've begun to win on Three of a Kind, and even a Club Flush on one memorable occasion. As with all things, the more you learn, the more enhanced the experience will be. Try **Criss-Cross**. It may not become your favorite, but be happy to have it as part of your Poker night!

Indian Poker

I've chosen to end the chapter with this ridiculous and sublimely funny variation on pure Poker, mostly because I have many fond memories of breaking out laughing during this very game. In **Indian Poker**, it's hard to keep a straight face — Poker Face or otherwise!

This is the ultimate bluffing game, and it can be played by anywhere from 3 to 10 players. It's probably one of the easiest Poker games to play, and one of the most theatrical. You get ONE card, ladies. And you stick it up on your forehead. I kid you not! And here is how the fun begins...

THE BUY-IN:

Each player pays a quarter into the Pot.

THE DEALER:

Deals one card down around the table.

PLAY:

Commences with each Goddess carefully sliding the card to the edge of the table without looking at it. If you peek, you have to pay a dollar into the Pot and are disqualified from playing out the rest of the game.

Once the card is there, you lift it up, it's top to your line of vision, which prevents you from seeing its value. Then, you hold it to your forehead. This makes your card visible to everybody else even though you can't see it, and their cards visible to you. Are you fighting back the tears of laughter yet?

As stated, **Indian Poker** is grand theater. Once each Goddess has assessed the cards held up to scrutiny on her fellow players' foreheads, betting begins to the Dealer's left and continues around the table with each player paying a dime into the Pot. Once all Goddesses have paid, everybody lowers their card. The High Card wins!

THE GOAL:

To be the holder of the Highest Card, and thus win the Pot.

A CHIC SAMPLE HAND:

Sandra has been dealt the Jack of Diamonds, but she can't see it because it's plastered to her forehead, out of sight! The best she can do is study the foreheads of her three gal-pals,

Yasko, Alibe, and the Fabulous Fiona. Fiona has the 10 of Clubs, the largest valued card around. Feeling confident, Sandra may wish to bet on the chance that her card is higher, and if she does, she'll win!

STRATEGY:

Indian Poker gained its name from the concept of 'scalping' — holding your card to your forehead for all to see. While in today's climate this may not seem politically correct, the game is nonetheless one to be experienced. It's fast, funny, and above all, fun.

In *Indian Poker*, since you can see everybody else's cards and know who has the highest, the best strategy for playing is based on that knowledge. If the cards are generally low value, there's a good chance yours might be higher, so bet like mad! If another player shows an Ace or King, it may be a good idea to fold. The key to this one exists in seeing what everybody else has and knowing not only who shows the Highest Card, but also what that High Card is!

Another, less concrete strategy is to quietly observe the reactions from your fellow Goddesses when they focus on your card. Do they balk or bet with abandon? If you can gage this, you might want to build your strategy around it. Besides its silliness, one of the beautiful things about *Indian Poker* is that it's a crazy, fast deal. It ends quickly, with the minimal amount of effort, and a maximum dose of chuckles!

CHAPTER THREE

In Addition To
Strip Poker...

For budding card enthusiasts, the universe of competitive games to be learned is a wide and wonderful one: Whist, Bridge, Hearts, Blackjack, Rummy — even games like Solitaire and Pyramid can be played should you find yourself alone, itching to deal the cards when no other Goddesses are around to join you at the table

This chapter focuses on several exciting competition games that are Poker's closest cousins on the evolutionary scale. Purists may balk, but we're sure you'll want to experience these lesser-known gems and welcome them into your circle of Goddesses. Quite simply, these fabulous games are smooth and sweet like a big stick of *buttah*.

Screw Your Neighbor

While we won't be covering the libidinous couple-favorite Strip Poker in this chapter of alternate and lesser-known Poker games, get ready to take a shot at a gem called *Screw Your Neighbor*.

Don't let the title fool you; this one is a great social game that can be played by up to ten people, and it's guaranteed to get your blood flowing. I have heard it alternately referred to as '*Stick* Your Neighbor,' which may be a more appropriate title given that the ultimate goal is to stick your fellow card players — your neighbors — with the crummiest cards in the deck while working to gain the High Cards, and to be the last one standing to claim the Pot. The game works best with three or more Goddesses seated around the Poker table, so prepare to sharpen your claws! This is how it's played:

THE BUY-IN:

Each player antes a quarter into the Pot. There is no betting in *Screw Your Neighbor*, however once the Ante is established, each player must then line up three equal piles of coin on the table in front of them, clearly displayed. To keep it pure, we will illustrate the piles at a value of ten cents each, which can come in the form of three dimes or any mix of nickels and pennies. Players in this game have Honors, meaning the three piles of coin actually total four — three physical chances to stay in the game, plus an invisible fourth that keeps the player alive once the last pile of coin is lost to the Pot.

THE DEALER:

Then deals down one card only to each of the players. Players may look at their card to see what they've been dealt but should keep it hidden from the competition.

PLAY:

Once all Poker Goddesses have assessed the card in their Hands, the action begins! The player to the Dealer's immediate left begins play, either keeping her card or passing it to the next in line and taking that player's card in exchange. Cards are valued King-high, Ace-low, meaning the crummiest card in the bunch, the Ace, and its cheap relatives the 2, 3, 4, 5, 6, and 7 cards are to be avoided like the plague. 8 cards and above are the best in this bunch! King cards dealt around the table are flipped face-up right away and placed on the table in front of the player who received it. This card, the ultimate in *Screw Your Neighbor*, cannot be taken from its holder.

If the first player holds a good, high-value card, she declares, 'Stay.' But if she has been dealt a dreadful low-value card and wants to exchange it, she may pass it to the next player in turn in the hope of swapping for a card of better value. The next player must switch with her unless she's been dealt a King (a flipped King card prevents an exchange from taking place with that player). If the first player switches a crummy card for an even crummier one, such as a 6 card for a 4 or a 2 for an Ace, the second player is now assured of a Higher Hand and may wish to then declare that she'll stay with what she's received, and hold off passing to the next in line, because she now risks getting an even worse card from the Goddess to her right. Why pass your card if you've already assured that it won't be you holding the lousiest value when the deal ends?

This exchange of cards continues in order all the way to the Dealer (and often with the old, "Here it comes!" declaration from the Dealer, who sees that lousy Low Card headed her way). Because play ends with the Dealer and the Dealer cannot pass on to the left, she may flip a single card to replace the one in her Hand if she so chooses. Once the pass of cards around the table ends, players show their cards upright. She who holds the Lowest Card must pay one of her piles of coin into the Pot. If Low Cards are matched by more than one player, all holding that card must pay. In other words, if the 3 card is the worst on the table and two of you each have 3's, both pay into the Pot. However, when the deal is down to two players, an equal flip of cards nullifies the round. Nobody pays, and a new Hand is dealt. Cards already played are then put face-down in a discard pile, and a new round is dealt from the deck.

The game continues in this manner, with each player trying to outmaneuver the others by getting the Highest Card in each round. The Dealer remains the same, unless she is knocked out of the game. Should that happen, the deal then passes to her left, and so on, until only one player remains with piles of coin or an Honor to her credit. And if you have enough players that you run out of cards before piles of coin and Honors, the Dealer shuffles the discards and the game resumes until a winner is declared.

THE GOAL:

To be the last player with coin on the table in front of her or to still have Honors. She who is left standing wins the Pot and the game.

A CHIC SAMPLE HAND:

Jenna draws a 6 card, an almost certain cue to pay. She should toss it to Angelica in the hope of catching a Higher Card.

STRATEGY:

On the surface, it would seem that both the first player to receive a card and the Dealer would have an unfair advantage to any players seated between them. But since all players at the table get two shots at bettering their Hand (in the card first dealt to them, and again in the card passed to their neighbor if they chose to take that chance), the odds of winning this game are pretty random, which is half the fun and frustration of *Screw Your Neighbor*.

A safe bet on trying to win this game is to hold the best card possible when possible, not always an easy thing when you're seated to the left of several of your best Poker friends. The first player to the left of the Dealer will want to hold onto an 8 card or higher, and pass on a 7 card or lower. Of course, you always run the danger of trading a 7 for a 6, or a

5 for a 2, or worse, the dreaded Ace (the kiss of death in this game, an Ace always pays). Knowing that all of the High Cards and junk cards might eventually be played based on how long the game goes means being aware of what's shown at the end of each deal.

Remember, the Queen is a great card, but it's sadly only the second greatest to the King (in this game, at least!). If you're the Dealer and the round comes down to you and a fellow Goddess who draws a King, even if you deal yourself a Queen, you'll still pay. As the Dealer, you must flip in the hopes of matching the King already on the table with one of your own. You may indeed do just that — stranger things have happened in this game! In a riotous recent match played by several friends, the rather large Pot was decided on a 3! The losing Goddess, sure she'd be able to best so pitiful a card, flipped an Ace.

She got screwed!

Grandfather

Ladies, since this is our book, we will hence refer to this easy-to-follow and enjoyable distant cousin to **Screw Your Neighbor** as **Grandmother**. Like **Screw**, **Grandmother** will tempt your senses and test your savvy, only in this entry, you are not only pitted against your fellow Poker Goddesses, but also an invisible presence seated at the table with you, the Grandmother Hand. To win, you will have to forget all those times Granny cooked Thanksgiving dinner, served you ice cream, or made you one of those fabulous fried egg sandwiches in her cast iron skillet. In **Grandmother**, she's a ruthless opponent heck-bent on making you pay up.

THE BUY-IN:

Each player antes a quarter (or higher as determined by the Dealer) into the Pot.

THE DEALER:

Then deals down two cards to each player. At the end of the deal, she deals the next three top cards in the deck into a separate pile. This is the infamous and deadly Grandmother Hand.

PLAY:

Once cards have been dealt, each Poker Goddess should look at her Hand and determine the value of what it is she's holding, keeping her cards hidden from the rest of the players. There are no Wild Cards in *Grandmother*. Aces are high, 2's low, so to hold an Ace or King means you've got a great Hand and should consider betting on it.

After players have assessed their Hands, the Goddess to the Dealer's left begins the betting or folding process. If she wishes to stay with her Hand, she bets another quarter into the Pot. For this, she receives a third card from the top of the deck to enhance the two already in her Hand. If she chooses to fold, she discards her cards face-down (folding in the game of *Grandmother* doesn't mean elimination from the entire match, just the round. More on this to follow after the really juicy stuff is explained!).

Betting or folding continues around the table, until all players have declared their intentions. Any player who bets is dealt a third card. Once betting concludes, all players remaining in the match lay their cards face-up on the table. She who holds the highest, best combination of cards (such as an Ace and Queen, or perhaps, even a Pair of 10's) could Potentially win the Pot —

But wait!

The Grandmother Hand remains to be seen!

Yes, that sweet, loving person who let you get away with murder when your own folks wouldn't can still trip you up and dash your dreams of claiming the Pot! In order to win the round, the top player must still beat the Grandmother Hand.

Once all players show their cards, the Dealer turns over the Grandmother Hand, revealing those three cards. If the top player holds an Ace-Queen-6 combination and the Grandmother's Highest Card is a Jack, the top player wins the Pot. Every other player who remained in the game must then match the value of the Pot, and the game continues, with the original Dealer passing the deal to her left. Any player who folded during the round now returns to the game and does not match the Pot.

If the Grandmother Hand shows a higher value, such as an Ace-King-2 or a natural Pair, the Grandmother wins. All players who bet must match the Pot, though any Goddess who knew when to fold them returns for the next round without having to pay.

The Dealer then passes deal to the player at her left. The game continues in this manner, with the Pot swelling larger and larger each time a round concludes. The game of **Grandmother** ends when only one player remains to face the Grandmother Hand, and bests it.

THE GOAL:

To outlast your fellow players and best the Grandmother Hand. She who refuses to fold and tackles the Grandmother Hand (and bests it!) wins the Pot!

A CHIC SAMPLE HAND:

Tasha has been dealt this wonderful Hand. She should hold it and take on the Grandmother.

STRATEGY:

Since there is no way of knowing what the Grandmother Hand holds, the player's best strategy is to go into the round feeling comfortable with her own cards. Being dealt an Ace or King in the initial deal of two cards is generally considered a strong enough reason to take on the Grandmother Cards, as well as face your fellow players.

Many times, by the luck of the draw, I've lifted my two cards to find a natural Pair. On other occasions, I've stayed in the game holding an Ace or King, only to be pleasantly surprised by the arrival of a matching card when the third is dealt to me. Of course, I've also bet on a Pair of Kings, only to have sweet, unassuming Grandmother turn up a Pair of Aces. Again, remember that in betting on a sure Hand, luck can sometimes be a lady while at other times, a heartless, thieving witch. Though it is quite possible to get Three of a Kind in your Hand (I've seen it happen rarely), a clean Pair of Aces will likely win you the Pot. I've also seen a friend of mine take the winnings in Grandmother on a deplorable, bare Jack-high Hand. While I don't condone violence in any form, later that night several of us contemplated slashing her tires and giving her a killer wedgie.

With several players matching an existing Pot, the amount of money at stake can swell quickly, so it is also a wise idea to set a personal limit in your mind on how far you're willing to go with this one. *Grandmother* is a great and tense game sure to provide hours of enjoyment for a friendly gathering of Poker Goddesses!

The safest and best strategy in playing *Grandmother* is to either trust in your cards or fold them. Just don't ever underestimate the Grandmother Hand — as much as we love our Grannies, after playing this game enough, you'll come to sympathize for the Wolf in *Little Red Riding Hood*, and understand why he devoured her.

Free Ride

Hop onboard! *Free Ride* is a simple and hilarious game that can be played by 3–7 players. Rounds continue until only one player remains at the table. Cards fly faster than cars at a racetrack, and there's a ticking clock element sure to keep you on the edge of your seat!

In *Free Ride*, the Dealer turns up cards around the table, and players pay into the Pot according to the value of their cards. Catching a Face card up is a free pass — you don't have to add to the Pot — at *first*. But get three Face cards or a Pair and you're eliminated from the game!

As well as being a great deal of fun, this is a pretty easy game to learn, so join the carpool and let's roll!

THE BUY-IN:

Each player antes a quarter into the Pot.

THE DEALER:

Flips cards up, one at a time, around the table, beginning to her left. She stops after each card is dealt to allow players to pay into the Pot.

PLAY:

In *Free Ride*, players pay into the Pot based on the face value of their cards. Cards are valued at:

♣ 2 — two cents
♦ 3 — three cents
♥ 4 — four cents
♠ 5 — a nickel
♣ 6 — six cents
♦ 7 — seven cents
♥ 8 — eight cents
♠ 9 — nine cents
♣ 10 — a dime
♦ Ace — eleven cents
♥ Jack, Queen, King are the 'Free Ride' cards, and will give you a free pass from having to pay.

Deal begins with the Dealer turning one card face-up to the

Goddess at her left. If that card is an 8, the player must pay eight cents into the Pot. Play continues to the next Goddess, who may get a 2 card. She pays two cents into the Pot. If the Dealer deals herself a Face card, she has gotten a free pass and pays nothing. The next round of play begins, and this is where the ride gets hairy!

Players begin to get eliminated from *Free Ride* any time after the second round commences, when the Dealer turns up the next card, laying it beside the one already dealt displayed in the first round. If a player already shows a 2 card down and another 2 card is dealt to them, she is eliminated from play. If players get a 10 card, they pay a dime into the Pot. Play then shifts to the next Goddess, who is dealt a card and is either eliminated by a Pair or pays the value of her next catch.

Play continues in this manner, as many rounds as it takes to eliminate all but the last Goddess who has yet to see a Pair up.

Players are only entitled to TWO free rides (a Pair of matching Face cards doesn't count you out). Should you get dealt a third Face card, you're eliminated from the game. Play ends immediately when there are two Goddesses left, and one of them is dealt a pair or a third Face card. The remaining Goddess then wins the Pot.

THE GOAL:

To be the last player on the table not dealt up a Pair or a third free ride card.

A CHIC SAMPLE HAND:

These are the first three cards dealt to Sydney. She'll pay a dime for the 10, a free ride on the Jack, and two cents for the 2 of Hearts. Sydney, just like good gal-pals Loretta Jane and Jenny Penny, will want to stay in this one to the end, since there is no way to tell who'll be the last lady standing until the cards have been dealt.

STRATEGY:

It's hard to offer much in the way of strategic planning in this one, since a player can't really prepare a Hand or engage her fellow Goddesses one on one. You are totally at the mercy of the cards in *Free Ride*, period.

The fun of this one comes through that random chaos — *who will survive the wrath of the Free Ride?* The only way to find out is to shuffle the cards, deal them, and drive!

31

There's nothing rare or obscure or even easy about this one, which employs multiple rounds and can be played by three or more of your card-wielding Goddess pals. In many card playing circles from coast to coast, the game of *31* is a classic! The reason behind its national notoriety has everything to do with the element of fast play, a certain amount of control over your cards, and the ability to formulate sharp strategies based upon them. There's also a level of complexity to *31*, but once you master this game, you'll love it. Many new Goddesses I initiated into my Poker circle threw their Hands up in confusion early on trying to learn this one because, as stated, there is a lot to consider in this game that only gets you three little cards. But now many of those same Goddesses consider this their favorite option to purer forms of Poker, and it remains the game played most on our wonderful and Wild card nights!

As with other games listed in this chapter, there is a ticking clock element to *31*, because the longer the round remains in play, the more likely it is that you or a fellow player will end up sticking it to the rest of the table.

There are three possible ways to win a round of *31*, but there are multiple rounds that must be survived in order to claim the spoils. Crack those knuckles and put on your best game face — you now have ice in your blood and a game of *31* to win!

THE BUY-IN:

Each Goddess pays a quarter into the Pot and then lines up three piles of dimes on the table in front of her, visible to all other players.

THE DEALER:

Deals three cards around the table to each player. She then puts the cards on the table and flips one up beside the rest of the deck, creating a discard pile. Players organize their three cards in order of suits or matching values, such as a pair of Kings, 8's, etc.

PLAY:

Play begins with the Goddess to the Dealer's left, who must decide whether she wants that flipped discard card, or the card off the top of the deck to augment her Hand. In *31*, there are no Straights, no Flushes. There are three different Hands a player strives to build in each round, and thereby set her opponents with. They are:

♣ The Highest Hand possible utilizing cards of the same suit (for example, three cards, all of them Hearts, Spades, etc).
♦ Three of a Kind such as three 8's or Kings.
☛ Or the ultimate Hand, 31, which is made up of the combination of an Ace and either two Face cards in the same suit, or a Face card and a 10 card. This is your high-yield weapon!

The first player takes either the discard or draws from the top of the deck. She then discards her worst card onto the TOP of the discard pile. The next Goddess does the same, and this continues on with each player trying to build the best Hand possible. You may only draw the top card off the discard pile. This can become maddening as the cards you're seeking get tossed face-up two players before you, and are thus considered boarded and untouchable!

If a player feels she has a decent High Hand — higher than her peers — she may wish to bring the round's final showdown, which will force the Goddess holding the Lowest Hand to pay into the Pot. In order to do this, she will have to make a declaration. That comes in the form of a KNOCK on the tabletop when the round again reaches her. She forfeits the right to draw another card from the deck and must physically knock on the table. This signals that the show-down is coming, and gives the other Goddesses one last chance to draw cards.

When play again swings around to the Goddess who knocked, she lays her cards down for everybody to see, stating out loud the numerical value of her cards. If her cards add up to 24, she says, 'Twenty-four.' Each Goddess does similarly.

Should you be savvy enough to build a Hand with Three of a Kind, you must also follow through with a certain etiquette before laying it down. Say you're holding a Pair of 7's, and the Goddess playing before you discards one onto the top of the pile. You may pick up that 7, and yes, you have one hell of a Hand now! But unlike the 31 Hand, which is laid down the instant you catch it, you will still have to wait one turn before showing your excellent Three of a Kind. Calmly take that 7 and toss the one card in your Hand that isn't a 7 onto the top of the discard pile, and wait for play to return back to you. Once it does, set your cards down onto the table. You don't have to knock with Three of a Kind. You just have to bide your time and hope nobody gets 31, because if they do, even with Three of a Kind, you must pay one of your piles into the Pot!

When you build a Hand totaling 31, as stated, you place it face-up before you immediately without waiting. Get that combination, raise your flag and drop the bomb. KABOOM! Everybody but you pays into the Pot.

In *31*, if the Three of a Kind or 31 Hands don't determine the round, the Low Hand pays a dime into the Pot. If two players are each holding the same low-Hand value after the

High Hand knocks — say an Ace and a 2 to total 13 — both players pay a dime into the Pot.

If you knock, thinking your combination of cards totaling 25 is good enough to best your peers, and they're holding 26, 29, or 30 points, you pay. Similarly, if you knock at 25 and your peers hold a matching 25 and above, you pay, not she with the matching Hand because you knocked.

Three of a Kind laid down in proper order makes every other player pay, unless somebody shocks you by setting down a higher-valued Three of a Kind. (This does happen! On rare occasions, right as you get ready to drop your three 10's, the player seated at your right drops three Jacks!)

When a 31 is dropped on the table, everybody pays into the Pot except the Goddess who unloads that Hand.

If you run out of cards before the round ends, the Dealer shuffles all of the discard cards except the last one showing (it becomes the base of the new discard pile), and play continues without interruption until somebody knocks or lays down Three of a Kind or 31.

Once the round ends, the deal passes to the Goddess at the original Dealer's left. Play continues around in this manner, with losing players paying into the Pot. Players have Honors in this game — the invisible fourth chance even after all three piles have been exhausted on the table. But once they lose Honors, they are out of the game.

Play ends when only one Goddess remains with either coin on the table before her, or Honors.

THE GOAL:

To be the last lady standing with either a pile or Honors. Do that, and you claim the substantial Pot — and bragging rights!

A CHIC SAMPLE HAND:

Sigourney catches the above Hand in a killer game of *31*. Her first instinct should be to search for good Clubs. She'll wish to lose the 2 and build her Hand up based on the Jack and 10 cards.

STRATEGY:

A common mistake made by beginners to *31* is in thinking that all cards in their Hand add up to make the count if somebody knocks. Only cards in a matching suit can be combined in that way, so if you have a good card to build on following the initial deal, such as an Ace or a Face card, it's usually prudent to hunt for cards to augment your Hand.

Much of what happens in *31* takes place soon after the initial deal, but this is one that can literally go to the bottom of the deck, with players changing strategies and dumping cards they later regret discarding. 'I broke up my Hand!' is often heard when a round lingers on. That's the nature of the beast!

That nature includes a predisposition to shed Low Cards early in a hunt for the highest ones in the deck, and there is a certain logic to it. If you're holding an Ace and a King of the same suit, and hunting for another Face card or the 10 of suit to reach 31, thus forcing the rest of your fellow players to pay, it is often prudent to hold onto even a lowly 3 card of the same suit if you draw it from the top of the deck. Such a combination would give you a total of 24 if somebody knocks.

At the other end of the scale, I've often taken a round by using a reverse approach: say I've been dealt a crummy 2 of Hearts in my initial cards. My turn to draw from either the top Community Card or the deck comes. I choose the deck and draw another 2 card — I now have 2/3rds of what I need on my way to getting a Three of a Kind Hand, which could Potentially set the entire table! And you can bet — as I often have — that anybody else who catches a 2 card will likely get rid of it quickly. That Goddess might be the one playing before me, and if she lays down that 2 on top of the Community Cards, I'm going to take it. I will have to wait yet another round before laying down my cards, but if given the chance, and if nobody else lays down a higher-value Three of a Kind or the highly-prized 31 combination first, I will have forced each player to pay a dime into the Pot.

Another strategy that has helped me win a round early on is by going on guts. If I catch good cards in the same suit early, two Face cards or an Ace-10 or Ace-Face card combo, I will knock without taking a card. This gives my fellow Poker Goddesses one last chance to catch a draw in the hopes of bettering their Hands and sends the room into a scramble.

Being quietly aware of what your fellow players are hoping to catch is another way to strategize your own method of play. How does one do this discreetly? By watching what is dumped and drawn from the discard pile. Of course, this is a great way to bluff out your opponents, by taking that 9 of Clubs the previous player discarded on the top of the pile and convincing your fellow Goddesses that you are hoping to catch Clubs, when you're really holding an Ace and 9 of Hearts.

Every time an Ace is discarded during *31*, the table holds its collective breath, for if the next player is holding a 10 and a Face card or two Face cards in the same suit, she will lay them down immediately on top of that Ace, making the dreaded and much sought-for 31 count. I've seen players hold onto Aces and Face cards just to prevent them from being utilized by another Goddess!

Of course, winning a round on a High Hand will only chip away at the piles of money on the table, whereas Three of a Kind and 31 Hands will slaughter the competition. Play *31* fair and smart, but play tough — and play to win!

99

This one remains a personal favorite — though the woman who taught us how to play it maintained it was one of her least favorite and often griped to the point of hostility each and every time the Dealer declared it was time to play, *'Noiyndy-Noiyn!' 99* is a counting game, in which cards build to a maximum numbered value, the aforementioned '99,' before three special cards reverse, hold, or end the Hand. Perfect for three or more players, it's a cutthroat little jewel of a game, in which the energy runs high and the cards fly fast — and it takes some smarts to win it, so please pay close attention...

THE BUY-IN:

Each player pays a quarter into the Pot and lines up three piles of dimes on the table in front of them, visible to all.

THE DEALER:

Deals each Poker Goddess three cards. Players then look at and organize their Hand, hopefully finding that fate has smiled upon them to include one or more of the following cards in the mix: the 8, 9, or 10 (more to follow on that!). Once players have their cards, the Dealer sets the remainder of the deck down at the center of the table. She does not flip up a top card to begin the play.

PLAY:

Cards in **99** have the following values:

♣ Aces = 1
♦ 2's = 2
♥ 3's = 3
♠ 4's = 4
♣ 5's = 5
♦ 6's = 6
♥ 7's = 7
♠ All Face cards (Jack, Queen, King) = 10

The fantastic game of **99** begins with the player to Dealer's left kicking things off by laying down one card, face-up, beside the deck. If the first player lays down a 7 card, she declares out loud, 'Seven!' Once she has discarded the 7, she

picks up the top card from the deck. Play then passes to the next player, who lays down atop the 7 and declares the value of her card in addition to what's been played. If she lays down a 6 card, she says, 'Thirteen.' She, too, draws the top card and adds it to her Hand. The next player follows. If she lays a Face card down, she must say, 'Twenty-three.' This continues, with players discarding and drawing, and the count of discarded cards building toward a magic number...
99.

Once 99 is reached, play takes a decidedly nasty turn. The count goes no higher — in this game, 99 is the maximum number the count may climb to. Should Poker Goddess #1 lay a Face card down when the count is 89, 99 is reached, and Goddess 2 can but hope that in her Hand of three cards, she has managed to catch an 8 card, a 9, or a 10. These are the magic cards!

♣ 8's will hold the count at 99 (or any other count for that matter).
♦ A 10 card laid on 99 will reverse it ten points, making the count 89 (the 10 card works in either direction — it can also be used to send a count of 89 up to 99, thus kicking off the scramble to survive!)
♥ A 9 card, played at any point in the game, automatically brings the count up to 99.

Once 99 is reached, play continues as long as there are cards being put down on the discard to support it. The first Goddess who runs out of playable cards ends the Hand and must pay one of the dimes on the table in front of her.

The deal passes on to the next player for a fresh round of cards. Play continues in this manner, with opponents trying to outsmart one another.

THE GOAL:

To be the last player with a pile of coin in front of you. There are no Honors in **99**. When all three piles have been paid to the Pot, you're out. She who stands last wins the game — and the cash!

A CHIC SAMPLE HAND:

Gates gets these on her first round of **99**. She should begin by ditching the Jack card. If a choice is to be made, the 2 should go next. The Ace should be kept along with any 9 or 10 cards unless Gates plans to accelerate the showdown.

STRATEGY:

I learned soon after our first attempts to play this game that a particularly cutthroat approach is the only way to succeed in **99**, and that means seizing opportunities when they present themselves.

The longer a Hand in **99** is allowed to continue, the greater the risk that your opponents will catch good cards from the deck. So if your Hand supports it, act!

If I've caught a 9 card early in the deal, I often lay it down immediately, because the odds are that not every player at the table has an 8, 9, or 10 in their Hand. This sassy act brings the count automatically up to 99, and the first person that doesn't have one of the magic cards to keep the Hand in play will have to pay up the Pot.

If you aren't dealt a Hand to support this, a good, less hit-and-run strategy is to quickly shed your Hand of any Face cards and to keep the lower ones in reserve as you try to gather 8's, 9's, and 10's from the top of the deck. An Ace or 2 can help you survive through another round once the count reaches the 90's. If it reaches 97 and you have a 2 in your Hand, you bring the count to 99 and survive to draw from the deck in the hope of catching a good card (this does happen!). An Ace in your Hand can save you similarly should the count reach 98 — if the player before you holds at 98 with their only useable card, an 8, you lay down the Ace and force the play to 99. Whoever follows you must lay down a magic card. This strategy thereby allows you to draw from the top of the deck to hopefully either catch an 8, 9, or 10, or force out another Goddess before play reaches you again.

Many times in **99**, the final Hand comes down to two opponents, each of whom have loaded their Hands with magic cards. One lays down a Face card on 89, brings the count to 99, then a grand duel commences, with 8's, 9's, and 10's flying onto the discard pile with the same sharp cracking sound as a gauntlet being thrown down. Like a white glove to a bare cheek, 99 will challenge you. You may hate it. My hope is you'll love it as intensely as I do. It's much more fun than Russian Roulette — and a whole lot less messy!

1-2–3 Dropout!

Another personal favorite destined to keep the room on its toes, *Dropout* found its way into our circle of friends on a warm May night not long ago. It quickly took on the stuff of legends among us both for its ability to build a Pot quickly to mammoth proportions, and also because few games depend on bluffing so highly as this!

It's a great game to be played by three or more Goddesses. In *Dropout,* you live and die by the initial cards you're dealt. There is no deal after that. What you see when you pick up that Hand is what you get. But just what you get is where the fun begins...

THE BUY-IN:

Each player pays a quarter into the Pot.

THE DEALER:

Deals three cards around the table to each Goddess. Players may look at their cards to assess them, and will want to arrange them with attention to:

♣ High Cards (Ace, King)
♦ Pairs
♥ A very rare Three of a Kind
♠ Or the best possible catch: a combination of both a 3 card and a 5 in your Hand. Any player who holds this combination automatically wins the Pot.

PLAY:

Once cards have been dealt and assessed, the Dealer brings the game to order by announcing in an authoritative voice, 'Ready!' This is a signal that you will soon decide whether to live or die by your cards. Having given your Hand the once over, each Goddess holds her cards out over the table face-down. The Dealer then says, '1 . . . 2 . . . 3 . . . Dropout!' At that moment, each player either drops their cards onto the table, a signal they are not willing to bet on the cards they've been dealt, or she holds them, meaning she and all others who didn't drop their cards will now reveal their Hands, hoping theirs is the best.

Those who have dropped out of **Dropout** remain active in the game, but are out of the round. Those who kept their cards square off, with she who holds the strongest Hand winning the Pot. Any bested player must then match the Pot. Once the Pot is paid, the deal passes to the Goddess at the original Dealer's left. She shuffles the cards, deals each player three cards, and the process repeats. Any player who dropped from the first round goes into this second round without having to pay again.

Play continues in this manner, with each Goddess trying to bluff her peers, and the stakes raising with every Hand (a one dollar Pot can quickly grow with three players trying to win it!).

♣ In the event that all players drop their cards at the Dealer's signal, everybody must pay the equivalent of their original Ante into the Pot.

♦ If two players stay in and each has the same High Card, she with the next highest card wins. If two players remain in with a Pair (for instance, a Pair of 7's), the player with the highest third card wins. On the unlikely chance that the players have the same third card (7, 7, and say, a King), the Hand is considered void and re-dealt. The same rule applies to more than one player with a 3 & 5 combination in their Hands.

♥ Play ends when only one person has held their cards after the Dropout signal is given. That player wins the last Pot and the game concludes.

THE GOAL:

To be the last Goddess holding her cards after her peers have dropped out, and thus collect the Pot's winnings.

A CHIC SAMPLE HAND:

Majel had drawn the magic combination, a 3 & 5 card. She will not drop out; the only Hand that can beat hers is a 3 & 5 combination with a higher than 9 third card.

STRATEGY:

The easiest advice for winning this awesome game involves looking at your cards, and quickly deciding whether or not you're willing to risk staying in with them. A player who catches a 3 & 5 combination will obviously want to remain in — the only way to lose is at the Hands of another player who's also caught a 3 and a 5, as well as a third card higher than yours. It happens, but infrequently.

A player who catches a Pair in her Hand in most cases should also risk staying in, because a Pair of anything will, in most instances, win the round! Of course, a Pair of 10's is going to beat out a pair of 3's. I've remained in the Hand with a pair of Kings, only to watch a friend lay down 2 Aces!

An Ace or King alone in reason enough to consider staying in the round. At the extreme end, I've watched brassy ladies win **Dropout** and walk away with the Pot on Hands that don't even contain a Face card, simply because they bluffed — and bluffed tough!

Acey-Deucey

In order to close our chapter devoted to the Wild and highly enjoyable cousins of the Poker Universe on a high note, we have purposefully left the game of *Acey-Deucey* to the end. Ladies, we are going out on a high note!

Hands-down, this is one of the neatest — and most frustrating — card games on the planet. It's a bidding game, and because the cards are used in a sparing manner to each player, it's an 'event' game that can be played by as few as three friends and as many as a dozen. There is only one Dealer per game of *Acey-Deucey* — but there is no clear single winner. Everybody has the Potential to win something in this game. They can also lose their shirts!

THE BUY-IN:

Each player pays a quarter or higher into the Pot (the more you ante with, the more exciting this game becomes). The Dealer must establish a minimum Bid. This can be any number, but cooler heads should prevail. The minimum Bid will affect everybody at the table and cause the Pot to grow exponentially, so you can make it a penny, nickel, dime, etc. The Dealer also needs to assign one of the players to keep score of the size of the Pot as it grows. This person, the Scorekeeper, will need a pen and paper, and will write this figure down before play begins. Your Scorekeeper *must* make sure to write down the increase/decrease of the Pot size so all will know exactly what is at stake as the game progresses. This is a fast-paced game so Dealer, Scorekeeper, and players need to keep up with the action!

THE DEALER:

Deals two cards up to the center of the table for all players to see, putting a few inches space between each card. These two cards are called 'Goalposts.'

PLAY:

In *Acey-Deucey*, Aces are always high, deuces low. Play begins to the Goddess at the Dealer's left. Those first two Goalpost Cards are hers, and seeing them, she must then bid, guessing on the value of the card the Dealer will flip up between the Goalposts. If the Dealer flips up a 4 card on one Goalpost and a Queen on the other, odds are pretty good that the Flip Card will fall between them — only a 2, 3, another 4 or Queen, and the King and Ace cards will set her. Should she flip from a 5 through a Jack, the player wins her Bet and may take it from the Pot.

But if the card flipped between the posts falls beneath the 4 or above the Queen, she must pay whatever her Bid is into the Pot. Also, if the Flip Card matches her Goalpost Cards, she must pay double her original Bid.

Play then continues on to the next Goddess in this manner, with the Dealer flipping up two new Goalpost Cards. The next player bids on those cards. The Dealer flips up a third card between them. If she wins her Bid, she takes her Bid from the Pot. If not, she pays. The game continues until reaching the Dealer, who flips her Goalpost Cards up, bets on them, and either profits or pays.

Acey-Deucey progresses around and around the table like this, with the Pot growing and shrinking.

♣ A Goddess cannot bet the value of the entire Pot until two full rounds have been played around the table.

♦ If the Dealer flips up impossible cards for the Goalposts (such as two matching Goalpost Cards, two 8's or two 10's, for instance; or an 8 card and a 7, creating the impossibility of catching a card between them), the player must make a minimum Bet and pay the Pot.

♥ The deck is reshuffled after all cards have been played, and play continues uninterrupted until the Pot is emptied.

THE GOAL:

To win as much of the burgeoning Pot and lose as little to it as possible.

A CHIC SAMPLE HAND:

Barbara gets the above two cards as Goalposts — what shall she do? The 5 cards and below, and the Jack and above cards are her bane; anything in between means profit. Barbara should play it safe and bet low. There will be plenty more rounds before **Acey-Deucey** concludes.

STRATEGY:

The payoff in this one has the Potential to swell to amazing proportions, for just when a player thinks she'll beat the Goalpost Cards and bets the value of the Pot, fate swoops down to remind her otherwise. This is a game of chance, and the cards don't always cooperate.

Many a time, I've seen a Goddess catch a decent Low Card and a High Card for the Goalposts, only to get slammed by the Flip Card. On the other side, I've seen some Wild bravado on a player's part, bidding between two Goalpost Cards like a 5 and a 10, and catching a 9 between on the flip to win the Pot!

While randomness plays a major part in **Acey-Deucey**, keeping a few basic strategies in mind can help increase your chances of winning this game. First, be aware of the odds. If you catch an Ace and a 2 card in the Goalposts, the only cards that are going to burn you are another Ace or 2. The likelihood of this is slim. Again, it does happen, but chances are against it.

When you're dealt lousy Goalpost Cards, make the minimum Bid and wait until the deal comes around to you again. *Acey-Deucey* is a game whose outcome is rarely decided quickly, so a good strategist will often be patient and observe, and strike when the opportunity presents itself. You'll get a minimum of two chances to win back your Ante, plus the Potential of a third round that goes at the very least to the first player at Dealer's left. Most times, play goes several rounds before the Pot is emptied.

While the cards can be cruel, it doesn't hurt to take a risk when you find yourself faced with a decent chance to win it all. Get an Ace, King, or Queen and a 3, 4, or 5 as your Goalpost Cards, the odds are in your favor you'll flip between them and make your bid. As the Pot grows and tension mounts, sometimes you just may find yourself faced with the decision to play safe, or risk it all. Close your eyes, take a deep breath, and if you sense the Poker spirits are currently smiling down upon you, go for it!

- ♣ ♦ ♥ ♠ -

CHAPTER FOUR

Poker Face

If one universal truth holds true in the game of Poker, it's that the odds were made to be broken. The element of luck is a magical and unpredictable force, and its presence at any Poker table is not to be overlooked anymore than those that are tangible, such as the number of players present and the addition of Wild Cards to your method of play. The game of Poker is a fine blend of heartbreak and triumph, of strategy mixed with a healthy dose of random chance, of the clearly visible and the veiled mysterious. Being not only aware of both facets but also embracing them on all levels can help sculpt a new card player into a bona fide Poker Goddess. Those concrete and abstract forces are the subjects of this chapter.

The Odds

We present the following Stats tables as mathematical examples only, for on many occasions, just when you're sure you will take a pot on your cards, somebody else will present the one hand out of the blue that can beat you. And at the other end of the spectrum, many times you will catch, seemingly from nowhere, the cards you need to win it all! This factor places the odds in a somewhat gray category that falls somewhere between the tangible and intangible.

5 Card:

♣ Royal Flush:	1 in 650,000
♦ Straight Flush:	1 in 72,200
♥ Four of a Kind:	1 in 4,200
♠ Full House:	1 in 700
♣ Flush:	1 in 510
♦ Straight:	1 in 250
♥ Three of a Kind:	1 in 48
♠ Two Pair:	1 in 21
♣ One Pair:	1 in 2.4
♦ High Card:	1 in 2

7 Card:

♥ Royal Flush:	0.0002 %
♠ Straight Flush:	0.0012 %
♣ Four of a Kind:	0.0240 %

- ♦ Full House: 0.1441 %
- ♥ Flush: 0.1967 %
- ♠ Straight: 0.3532 %
- ♣ Three of a Kind: 2.21128 %
- ♦ Two Pair: 4.7539 %
- ♥ One Pair: 42.2569 %
- ♠ High Card: 50.1570 %

THE CONCRETE

Touch it, feel it, see it — or read it! These are tangible elements that will help improve your game of Poker!

BETTING WISELY

Most Poker gurus will tell you that as a general rule, it's good to show up to the table with at least 20 times more than the cost of a single game — and even better to outfit yourself with up to 50 times more! If a round of **Anaconda** ends up costing you three bucks, make sure you have at least sixty on hand in your bankroll for the games that follow or else it could end up being a pretty early night!

Having that bankroll means using it wisely to make the most profit possible, so if your cards support taking a risk on them, do so. If not, fold, and wait for the next game. No Poker player wins every single deal of the cards. You will lose some of them, but if you play wisely, you'll find yourself hauling in some nice Pots, too!

In friendly card games played around my kitchen table, oftentimes one Goddess has helped out another when her bankroll quickly vanished into a vortex of bad luck. We've jokingly referred to this extension of credit as 'The Lending Library' — 'Don't worry, Laura, darling — the Lending Library is open.' If one of us has exhausted our Poker money, we graciously extend a few dollars credit in the direction of our poverty-stricken fellow card maiden, knowing fully well she will repay it the instant she wins something back.

Of course, this policy won't apply to you in a professional tournament or casino, so learn how to manage your bankroll on a friendly level. Spend it wisely as you would on any investment, aiming for the minimum of loss, and the maximum of gain!

POKER FACES

In many ancient cultures, tribes of mighty warriors went into battle wearing elaborately painted masks as added intimidation. The tradition can still be seen in modern-day competitive sports. Pitchers in Big League Baseball often don't shave on days when they take the mound, knowing that the rough stubble on their faces lends an extra element of fear to the enemy. The same holds true for football and hockey players, and one needs only look in the direction of the goalie's helmet to see that the 'game face' is not only alive and well — it's looking pretty scary in the 21st Century!

Poker players, too, should prepare similarly for battle. This facial enhancement to the exterior persona is commonly known as the Poker Face, and each Goddess displays hers differently. Some like to wear their emotions on their sleeves, while others prefer the poetic simplicity of an icy smile.

As a point of personal choice and business savvy, I extol

praise to that Goddess who sits calm and collected in her seat, showing neither disinterest nor too much emotion once the cards have been dealt to her. A smart Goddess studies her cards without tipping off her fellow players to their value. She remains coldly efficient before, during, and after the deal. And please remember that a player who gloats with obvious flair after she's caught a winning Hand isn't likely to remain popular for long. Nobody likes a braggart!

Decorate that war mask however you want. Just know that your opponents are seated across the table looking for any sign of a crack in your armor.

KNOWING THE GAME

As in everything one hopes to master, whether it involves growing a garden, cooking the perfect quiche, or performing brain surgery, the best way to be successful is to study as much available information on the subject as possible. The same holds true for Poker. If you want to succeed at the game, learn all you can learn, especially from those who mastered it before you.

A plethora of excellent books currently exists on the subject. A quick scan through the shelves of your local bookstore or library can help, as will logging on to your computer and surfing the Internet to either Amazon.com or Barnes & Noble Online to see what is currently available. A recent perusal through Amazon.com using the keyword 'Poker' lists over 300 results, a number sure to grow with every year!

Poker-themed books range in scope from practical handbooks for the beginning card enthusiast to advanced strategy guides, even Poker murder mysteries for the

Goddess who needs a little light reading at the end of the day once she's cleaned out her fellow players! A host of instructional videos are also available through online bookstores.

The quintessential trade magazine on the subject, *Poker Digest*, is another valuable resource for budding and seasoned Poker Goddesses. Every month, PD offers a variety of fresh news, instructive articles, and industry information, as well as updates on professional Poker tournaments (such as the Crown Jewel of the Poker circuit, The World Series of Poker) and Poker cruises. The online version, which can be accessed at *www.pokerdigest.com*, also carries links to some of the finer Poker websites.

ONLINE RESOURCES

The Internet offers scads of information for the Goddess who wishes to acquaint herself fully with the entirety of the Poker Universe.

By doing a general search using the keyword 'Poker' on any good search engine, you will encounter the plethora of online Poker gaming sites promising easy money and instant riches. Like other, more adult-oriented sites for which the Internet has become notoriously renown, let the buyer beware!

A fabulous resource to Poker Goddesses can be found at *www.pokerpages.com*, the premiere website for the woman enthusiast. Considered the Number One Poker portal for women on the web, more than 120,000 visitors log onto Pokerpages.com every month. The site's web mistress, Tina Napolitano, has pulled together a massive amount of excellent material, including interviews with some of the premiere lady card players on the planet. It's a great, safe place to gather with other players who abide by a code of ethics and fair play. The site boasts a chat room and actual online Poker gaming where new Goddesses can practice playing for free. It is also home to PokerSchool.com, the world's only school devoted to teaching players ways to better their game from both ethical and winning perspectives.

THE ABSTRACT

These are the mysterious and magical, the winsome and slightly absurd elements of Poker. They are felt and seen with the inner eye, and though not as tangible as other facets of the game, they should never be fully discounted.

GOOD LUCK CHARMS

For many years, Anna, one of the loveliest ladies I've ever had the pleasure to play cards with, carried a separate purse for her special coins. This purse sat beside the rest of her bankroll on the table, but its contents were never, ever to be used. These pennies, nickels, and dimes were the ugliest, most demented coins found anywhere on the planet! One penny had been mutilated on the train tracks so badly, Lincoln's head was stretched and flattened to twice its normal size. One was splattered with white paint and thus earned the nickname, 'the Pigeon Crap Penny.' Among them was a penny painted red — the quintessential red cent — a quarter painted blue, some old buffalo head nickels, wheat pennies, and other coin oddities.

These were Anna's good luck charms, and in our card-playing circle, they became the stuff of legends! I'm not sure that they ever truly helped Anna win at Poker, but so it goes with talismans. They work only to the degree in which we give them our faith.

Our personal good luck charm is a Christmas ornament given by a friend the year G. L. and I wrote episodes of the television series, *Star Trek: Voyager*. It's in the shape of *Voyager's* stalwart Captain Janeway, and on many times, it has sat on the table near our bankrolls, peeking across the cards at our opponents, often to their chagrin. One such frazzled Poker player was known to declare, "She's staring at me! Would you please turn her toward somebody else?"

Psychological warfare had not been the intention, but we did clean up that night. Naysayers will likely just chalk it all up to skill and sound Poker tactics, though part of us believes it may have been the luck of the Irish!

PRE-GAME RITUALS

In games played around your kitchen table or at the homes of friends, you might find yourself developing certain pre-game patterns. For whatever reasons, that's what competitors do when going into battle. Everyone knows the stories of baseball players who wear the same pair of 'Lucky Socks' that won them the big game, or of players who dress in their uniforms a certain way every time, or eat certain foods before taking the field for that first inning. The same may hold true for you and your buildup to the big game!

When Goddesses are expected at my home, I light candles and then run through a set of pre-game rituals to better my own game once the cards are ready to be dealt. I spend half an hour or so seated at the Poker table with a notebook and pen in hand, and I write. This helps me clear my mind of all other work-related information. I jot down notes, deadlines, and anything else necessary to my life at that time, and once it's all down on paper, I effectively put these distractions from the largest part of my life out of my Poker game. By the time my fellow Goddesses arrive, I am coldly focused only on the cards and ready to play my best.

During breaks for drinks or dessert, I will sometimes run through the notes I jotted down an hour or two before to repeat the process if I feel my mind has wandered. Once the cards are ready to be dealt, I close the notebook, clear my mind, and it's down to the work at hand. This is my personal ritual, and it has helped me stay focused in both my Poker and business lives.

Two summers ago, during a particularly stressful time when the demands of work seemed to double, I was taking notes on a small, hot-pink notepad whose color, for whatever reason, drove my dear friend Anna insane with rage. Just to see it balanced on my tiny corner of the Poker table launched her into a fit of, 'there you are with that darned *pink thing* again!'

That I kept winning during that stressful time was cause enough for me to keep jotting down the notes about my writing work on the hot pink notepad. I continued to use that pad right down to the very last sheet, and to this day, the 'Legend of the Pink Thing' still gets bantered and replayed around our table.

You, too, will find strange and whimsical practices to better your play — and you may find yourself returning to them each time the promise of gathering with your fellow Goddesses for a night of cards arises!

GROUP RITUALS

As with personal rituals, your circle of Goddesses may find itself indulging in pre-game group practices to enhance an already wonderful experience.

Since forming our Poker group, we Goddesses who've never needed much nudging when it comes to gathering in the name of food — often break bread with a hearty pre-game meal. It has become something of a ritual of goodwill. One of us will cook the main course. Another will bring fresh bread. Somebody else provides a delicious dessert.

On occasion, I have made a boiled dinner or smoked shoulder with the vegetables. Anna has treated us all to a night of homemade lasagna or manicotti with warm garlic bread, and if that wasn't enough, a scrumptious chocolate cake with coffee to follow.

One of my favorite group rituals is to set the Poker table with all the essentials: a brass holder filled with good cigars for whoever wants one, glasses for soda or champagne, and a tray of cookies or other decadent treats. Our favorite group Poker rituals almost always involve these 'Three Cs': Champagne, Cigars, and Chocolate!

No matter how you set your Poker table, always come to it ready to play fair and tough, and above all, enjoy the challenge that awaits you. If and when you are ready to take the savvy you develop here to the next level, you'll know it.

And once you have...

Gentlemen, look out!

- ♣ ♦ ♥ ♠ -

CHAPTER FIVE

Wendeen Eolis:
Interview with a True
Poker Goddess

Few Poker Goddesses are as successful — or colorful — as Wendeen Eolis. A true inspiration, Wendeen was the first woman to finish in the money in the prestigious World Series of Poker in 1986. A decade later, following her second record-setting performance for a woman in the final event, the casino that created the tournament, Binion's Horseshoe, issued a WSOP commemorative Poker chip in her honor.

By day (and her days often stretch well into the night!), Wendeen is the CEO of a highly successful law practice consultancy that specializes in the selection and review of lawyers, law firms, and legal services worldwide. She is also the former First Assistant and Senior Advisor to New York Governor George E. Pataki, and a former Special Advisor to New York City's celebrated Mayor, Rudy Guiliani. Additionally, Wendeen served as a consultant and has vetted counsel prospects for the federal government under Presidents Ford, Reagan, and Bush in connection with Federal and State Gaming issues.

In addition to her legal business and Poker adventures, Wendeen is a classical pianist who as a child performed as a soloist at New York City's famed Carnegie Hall. She has also appeared on television as a co-anchor on Court TV, and was featured on A & E's Biography Close Up Special on the game she has both grown to love and master, Poker.

Wendeen recently parlayed that mastery and her many incredible Poker experiences, and victories into her forthcoming book, *Power Poker Dame.* On the night we met Wendeen, as a testament to her endless energy and enthusiasm, she was simultaneously organizing an event for survivors of the September 11th Tragedy in New York City, and planning a trip to Europe to research her favorite casinos for the writing of her book, and a special feature story for *Poker Digest*, the industry's pre-eminent Poker magazine. And as a credit to her radiance, despite her demanding schedule, she was never too busy to give us a great deal of her precious time — and even more of her wisdom.

We present to you the success story of Wendeen Eolis, Poker Goddess!

Tell us more about you — just who is Wendeen Eolis?

I was born in 1944 to Russian immigrant parents, both of whom were lawyers. They were incredibly bright and ambitious. They both worked very hard and relied in large measure on governesses and housekeepers for my upbringing while they enhanced their careers and provided for our family. I was raised and schooled in more places than I care to remember, but New York was and still is my primary base.

You have a pretty amazing life outside of Poker. Could you share with us some of those amazing complexities, including your legal counsel work for former New York City Mayor Rudolph Guliani and New York Governor George Pataki?

In 1969, I founded the first EOLIS legal consultancy as a legal recruiting and executive search firm. Today, as the Chair and CEO of Eolis International Group, Ltd., I oversee the operations and policies of the company which specializes- through its five service divisions — in the employment and review of lawyers, law firms, and legal services worldwide. I established EOLIS as the first search firm exclusively for practicing attorneys. The company evolved into its current international legal consulting practice to assist law firms and corporate law departments, and clients of legal services, including company boards, and government agencies.

Then I got involved in attorney research, specifically market trend studies of the legal profession and due diligence reports related to the credentials, experience and reputations of individual lawyers and partner groups. I extended the practice to law management consulting which meant helping those law firms and the law departments of companies with regard to such matters as their internal structure and compensation, and internal relationships. From there, I got into the part of the business that is both most unique and best known in my operation: reviews, selection, retention, and changes with respect to a client's outside legal counsel.

The other part of my business in which I have developed a special niche is the career consulting work that I do with lawyers who seek political office and government officials who want to return to private practice, as well as more traditional candidates — partners in law firms and senior corporate lawyers — looking for substantive transitions.

My interest in politics began at home with my stepfather, a highly placed politico in New York State government. It increased during my tenure as the president of a trade association during the mid-70's. Then it zoomed forward as a result of my contact with Mayor Rudolph Giuliani in the late 70's when I first met him at the law firm of Patterson, Belknap, and Webb, the firm I recommended to the *Chicago Tribune* for a new legal matter. Rudy Giuliani was a young partner. Shortly after Rudy joined the firm, we were introduced and as a result of my continuing to work with both the *Chicago Tribune* (and its subsidiary the *New York Daily News*) and Patterson, Belknap, & Webb as clients, Rudy and I became friends.

Rudy and I talked intermittently during his Washington days. We talked about his political and private sector ideas and objectives. Shortly after Rudy met his second wife, Donna, and he returned to New York, as United States Attorney for the Southern District, there was more opportunity to be in touch again, and eventually Rudy's entire family treated me as if I was an extension of it. Rudy and Donna and their children and their relatives, and friends became a wonderful part of my life.

By 1988, when Rudy was thinking about leaving the U.S. Attorney's Office to run for elective office, I was one of the key people to whom he turned to share his vision and consider alternatives. By 1989, I was firmly ensconced in Rudy's campaign for the

Mayoralty. The period between 1989 when he lost the election and '93, Rudy was a political student and so were all of us who called ourselves close friends.

In 1993, I started to take politics seriously. It's a good thing that I did since Rudy won the election and I became a member of his Mayoral Transition Team!

During the first several months in 1994, I had the good fortune of being a regular visitor at City Hall while maintaining my business. During that year, I had an opportunity to give advice or more accurately to be a sounding board on City Hall operations, particularly in regard to personnel, the law department, and the city's press office. I often sat in on the highest level meetings and enjoyed the unique position of an insider with considerable access to the Mayor and an opportunity to provide input on appropriate subjects.

Then, in July of 1994, I was reintroduced to another lawyer I had met in his earlier days, George Pataki. The gubernatorial candidate was anxious to get on the same page as the Mayor and looked to all of Rudy's friends for support. I fit the mold of friend, so I was among those he looked to for that support. Ultimately, the Mayor supported Governor Pataki's opponent in that election. I threw my support to Candidate Pataki with exuberance and independence from the Mayor in my decision. When George Pataki was elected, he made me an offer I could not refuse as his First Assistant and Senior Advisor. The job of First Assistant meant being available to take responsibilities and assignments as he developed them. As his Senior Advisor, the two major issues in my portfolio were gaming matters, both private sector and Indian gaming regulations, and related legislation, and the other hot potato of the moment, which was rent deregulation.

The period in which I was in the Executive Chamber would have been a heady experience if I had just been a fly on the wall. But actually, I got to be a bit more than that in the course of being the Governor's representative with various state officials, business and civic leaders, as well as in the one-on-ones that were called for in my position which reported directly to him.

Tell us more about your home life.

For years, I have maintained a significant amount of privacy about my personal life. But I am happy to tell you that I have three chosen children and enjoy the fruits of their labor in eight grandchildren. I have been married more and less formally (under common law more times than I discuss) and have loved well. One part of my life that is an open book is my deep attachment to Lexis, my 2-year-old miniature blue merle Sheltie who resembles my childhood blue merle collie. I recently lost Counsel, my four-pound Maltese, who gave me and everyone else around him 15 years of unconditional love.

How did you first become interested in Poker?

I became interested in Poker somewhat by accident. I was playing Backgammon socially at the time, and there was a Poker game going on in the corner of the same clubroom. I told myself that I had 'card sense' — I had been a Blackjack counter during my days in college. So I picked up a Poker book, one of the only Poker books available at the time. It was called *Super System*. I barreled through that book and concluded that I was ready to become a professional Poker player.

I kid you on that, because the last thing I expected to become was a professional Poker player. I ambled over to the table where they were playing and watched on a couple of evenings for a few minutes here and there between my Backgammon games. Finally, 'No-Fear Eolis' showed up at the table and the players happily ushered me to a seat knowing that I was going to be the tenth best player out of the ten players in the game. I backed away from that challenge and got back to Backgammon. But a few months later, with a couple of trips to a resort hotel that offered Poker and where I really learned the basics of the game, I was back at the Backgammon club with that Poker table in the corner, ready to play the biggest game in town. Lo and behold, on my very first night, I had beginner's luck and hauled in a win worthy of one of the pros! But what I failed to win was the respect of any of the other players. Instead, the good-looking guy sitting next to me told me I was sitting in the wrong game and should scat. I looked at him as if he was from another planet, wondering how he dared to question my Poker prowess when I had just hauled in one of the biggest pots of the night!

Over the next couple of years, he explained it all to me at the Poker table, the coffee table, the dining room table, and in more private places. My mentor became my lover and my best friend. It was an incredibly exciting adventure and during the period we were together, I cannot remember our ever having an argument until the very end, which was short and certain, when both of us returned to our former life partners.

Did people in your family play cards when you were growing up?

My stepfather played Poker from the time he was twelve. When I was growing up, every year he had a summer Poker party, which was how I was introduced to the game. I would help to get the tables ready for the Poker barbecue. But that was about it for me, as a kid.

Though I knew very little about Poker as a child, I did know a lot about cards in general. Everybody in the family played cards — War,

Casino, Canasta, Gin Rummy, Hearts, Pinochle, and I'm sure a bunch of others I no longer remember. I was the very best at every one of them, except at Bridge, which to this day I don't even consider, probably because my mother was such a successful player and I could never beat her.

When it came to games, I was the Queen of Monopoly, Clue, and others also with names that have long since been forgotten, but there is no doubt that I was a strong competitor in every facet of my family life which rubbed off early, into student life as well.

Competition and competitiveness were threaded through my childhood in both positive and negative ways. The competitive spirit ultimately resulted in the independence that made it possible for me to jump away from family life at the age of fifteen, when I started to live on my own.

While in college, my interest in cards took a substantial turn into the world of Blackjack after I read a book by an MIT professor on how one could beat the game. I promptly set about learning effective counting strategies and after significant success as an independent player, met up with a man who eventually became my Blackjack partner and my children's best friend, while reserving enough time for me on the side. He went on to become the world's best known Blackjack player, while I retreated into the more conventional world of business.

How did you journey from playing friendly card games to becoming one of the First Ladies of professional Poker?

The truth is I have never thought of Poker as a friendly game. It is a serious income-producing hobby and a burning passion. I have never taken my hobbies casually! I've always wanted to be the best that I can be, and do the best that I can do, which accounts for why tennis and driving are rarely part of my activities, though I own both a tennis racket and a car.

What are your favorite variations on Poker?

In Poker, my favorite games are No Limit Texas Hold 'em and Pot Limit Omaha. They are both known as big bet Poker games in which you better learn how to play mistake free or you won't be playing for long.

Do you have a memory of a favorite individual card game either with friends or as a pro, a time when something funny, wild, unexpected, or insane happened?

There are so many favorite stories, but from a woman's point of view, one of the funniest and also one of the most gratifying early Poker experiences came about during a major tournament. I was sitting at a table at which almost every other player was a pro and it was a No Limit game, no less! I was playing my heart out and still scared to death of every hand, when I picked up a respectable Pair of Jacks. My opponent tried to intimidate me by drawling, *'How much more money do you have, ma'am?'* I politely answered, *'You may ask the Dealer to count me down.'*

So this Texas gentleman immediately pounced on the dealer to count me down for all my chips, and he said, *'Honey, put it all in.'* I told him I didn't have to decide about that until he'd made his decision about whether he was putting money in since he was the bettor. In an instant, he placed his money in the center of the table. I did the same, sure in my mind that he was just trying to intimidate me, and that he had a decent Hand, but not a Hand as good as mine. When we turned over our cards the audience could see our respective hands, and when it turned out that my Jacks were the winners over his Pair of 10's, the spectators broke out in the loudest cheers.

That Hand put him out of the tournament. I thought that was terrific, and I was still reeling from the thrill when another gentleman walked over to the table to the vacant chair. He looked at me as he sat in the seat of the player who'd just been ejected from the tournament, and he said, '*Well, honey, I guess we'll be playing a few Hands today.*' Another player at the table looked up, as did the tournament director, and in unison, they said, '*The last guy who called her that isn't here anymore.*' I think that was the last time I feared facing anybody in a Poker game. I always think of that story because it turned the tide on people being able to bully me in a Poker game!

What is the weirdest thing you've ever seen or experienced at a Poker game?

There are so many things that have happened at one time or another, but one extraordinary event at a Poker game was a police raid in the middle of New York City in a private card room that the authorities deemed illegal. But the extraordinary part of the experience when we were raided was not that the cops came in, but that the first cop I encountered, said, '*Hold up!*'

I mistakenly thought we had just become the victims of an armed robbery. I turned my head around, marched back into the clubroom, took a seat at a table and put my head down for fifteen minutes while they gave orders to a few of the players, never realizing that it was a police raid until I again raised my head! All of the conversations had sounded exactly like it was a hold up. It was the most amazing, weird experience. After hearing the words 'Hold up!' these plain-clothed law enforcement officers told everybody to sit down and be quiet, then they asked one or two people to show their identification, and threatened to cause big problems if anyone moved. Then they said they'd make examples of us if we didn't cooperate. It felt like an hour, though in actuality, it was only a matter of minutes. When I raised my head and saw uniformed law enforcement agents with police jackets in the crowd I was so relieved! Moments later, they let us leave and told us not to bother coming back. They realized we were a crowd of social players with regular day jobs and families instead of gun-toting, racketeering, narcotics-carrying desperadoes.

Regrettably in New York City, it's not legal to play Poker. So Poker games, which sprout up in all the boroughs, are always subject to investigation by the police, and in recent years, raids have become increasingly frequent. This discourages people from playing in the city. Many travel to places like Connecticut's Indian gaming facilities and to Atlantic City.

Do you have any rituals?

That's a really interesting thing that you ask because in *Power Poker Dame*, I explain that I treat the Poker room like it's my office. It begins with my setting up a small side table next to me for drinks and magazines I may want to take a look at. I set my chips in amounts and stacks in a particular way, neatly in rows. I keep a cell phone handy, because who can be in the office without reporting to their nearest and dearest at home? And there are probably a whole lot of other things that are part of my routine, if not exactly rituals during the course of a Poker game. Clearly, I try to create an environment that makes it easy to do my work. Keep in mind you have to be pretty ingenious since your space at the Poker table doesn't extend beyond your hips. Of course, over the years, my hips have extended beyond that usually allotted skimpy space!

Do you have a good luck charm?

No, no good luck charms, but I do have the 20th anniversary silver bar that I acquired at the World Series of Poker, and I use the commemorative chip that the wsop issued in my honor, in 1996, for my achievement on behalf of women.

How much money have you earned on the pro circuit?

As far as I am concerned, Poker earnings are a private matter, and as befits a lady I prefer privacy with respect to the details of my personal affairs. I consider these earnings as I do the earnings from my privately held company: information to be shared on a need-to-know basis, only.

Where do you like to play cards — Las Vegas? Atlantic City?

While I have played in various private club settings in the New York City area, I prefer public card rooms. During the summer, it's nice to have a Poker weekend either in the mountains of Connecticut or by the ocean in Atlantic City, but the best Poker room as far as I am concerned is the one in which I am winning. I find it easier to focus on Poker when I can leave the office worries behind and truly enjoy the game such as I do at the fabled wsop.

Do you have a favorite Las Vegas casino?

I love Bellagio. It is a beautiful hotel with equally elegant guest-rooms. I have a tremendous number of friends there. Bellagio's Poker room is very comfortable and well managed, and boasts some of the best fast-paced action anywhere in the world.

By the way, I adore a Poker room where I'm not only winning, but also meeting good friends.

What was it like the first time you entered a casino to play Poker?

The first time I ever entered a casino, I was accompanied by one of the world's most successful and highly regarded Poker players, so it was something of a social event — and a coming-out party so to speak — with the man in my life who was always center stage when he walked into a Poker room. Had he not accompanied me, I am sure I would have felt a bit overwhelmed, wondering how to get into a game, whether to be quiet or friendly at the table, etc. But I would undoubtedly try to handle it like I do most new situations; summoning the full range of curiosity and excitement to help me overcome any natural fear.

In actual fact, however, things went a bit differently on my first solo sojourn, which was at a resort hotel. I parked myself at the first chair to which I was directed and made myself part of the game. None of the pros and unknowns seated around me realized for about ten seconds that I was a total newbie. But once they did, my emerging Poker persona fell flat on its face and it took weeks for me to develop self-confidence at the table, as I learned quickly that these folks were seasoned pros.

What should a hopeful Goddess be aware of when moseying up to a casino Poker table?

First and foremost, before sitting down at a table in the Poker room, she must know the basics of the game, including the specific card game she chooses to play. She needs to know the language of the game — Poker room nomenclature, the idioms and the slang, otherwise you will sometimes find yourself out in the cold. These days, it's vital to read, selectively, the available books written about the games of your choice; practice in small stakes live home games that include people at your level and a little bit more, and a little bit less knowledgeable than you (the best prescription to try to win and learn at the same time); and by all means, click your computer mouse onto Pokerpages.com and sign up for their Poker School Online, which provides serious tutoring to improve your game. Only after you've done all three of these things should you venture into a public Poker room and face the music by yourself.

How have men reacted to your presence at the Poker tables?

The reactions of men are quite variable. Poker remains a male-dominated game. There are still men who are resentful of having a woman present, and not only seated there at the Poker table, but also winning at it! Some men express this resentment at the table with language better suited to the locker room; occasionally it is a deliberate act to throw a lady off her game. Even the best-monitored Poker rooms do not always protect delicate ears!

With this forewarning in mind, Poker ladies are enjoying increasing respect in public Poker rooms largely through enlightened Poker room managers who are going to great lengths to market the sport to women, and to make a beginning Poker

Goddess feel just like one at least with respect to camaraderie, professionalism, and respect among players and personnel. In fact, in games where pro Poker players and regulars congregate, the conduct tends to be very much like what you would expect in any environment of competition where camaraderie is still very much a part of it. So is basic courtesy. It should also be said, that in a Poker room as on the street, when a 20-something buxom type of Goddess with flowing blonde hair arrives, the 'tart' type, most men turn their heads to see. But no Goddess should get too cocky and pay too much into that type of distraction once she gets into her chair at the table. It doesn't take long for the pros to turn their heads back in the direction of the cards to watch women as well as men strictly in terms of how they play their chips.

Please share with us your amazing experiences as a champion at the World Series of Poker at Binion's Horseshoe Casino.

In 1986, I became the first woman to 'finish in the money' which means to earn a share of the purse at the biggest Poker event in the world. And the second time I cashed in the final event, I was nine days away from going into the hospital for a major surgery. In both cases, they were record-setting performances for a woman and so, of course, I was proud of the achievement and found myself enjoying the fifteen minutes of media fame that invariably follows in these circumstances. However, from the moment I was eliminated from the competition, I began thinking about the next year's event.

Today, ten years later, there are a significant number of women who have passed my individual accomplishments. Business and political commitments as well as attending to my health have resulted in my giving up most tournament play. But I continue to pound the live game big bet tables from time to time throughout the year and have retained one of the highest percentages of money finishes (among men and women) in the few tournaments I have tackled. In the World Series of Poker, there are only five women who've ever come in as money finishers twice, and I am quite thrilled to be among them! The World Series is the one tournament that means the world to every serious Poker player. It draws media from around the globe. It's at this event that I continue to find myself something of a media magnate, which is part fun, part fury, and part fright. So was the case last year when *The New York Times* dispatched a reporter to follow my every move from the day I arrived to the tournament to the moment the last hand was dealt. It was an experience to remember — but also one not to replicate!

At the World Series of Poker, you must remember that you are there to play your very best game and to win. And your best effort, despite the excitement that infuses the World Series, means keeping your focus. In fact, the experience with the reporter was very instructive in teaching me a tough lesson; I'm now convinced that the reporter's constant presence at close range was seriously distracting to my efforts in a multi-million dollar proceeding. Next time out I'll be keeping my eye on the ball, not on the flack! When you're playing Poker, chat another time, primp another time, stay focused on the business at hand.

What is the most important lesson you've learned on this journey?

I've learned many lessons playing Poker. *Power Poker Dame*, the book I'm writing, is a series of Poker adventure stories that highlight invaluable lessons: the life experience I have brought to the game, the battles I have fought in the Poker rooms, and the lessons that I have bought at card room Poker. But no lesson is more important than Shakespeare's relevant words: *To thine own self be true.*

I've learned that bluffing is an overrated strategy in business, politics, and especially in Poker. Women can win more money by bluffing less. This single premise is central to the development of my style of play. Simply stating the obvious, I prefer to play with a good Hand rather than rely upon bluffing with weaker ones. Quite remarkably to the initiated, Poker is not all about bluster and guts but rather the art and science of the 'semi bluff,' which in real life we refer to as calculation of 'potential' as well as the facts in front of us.

Why do women make not only good but also great Poker players?

One characteristic found more frequently in women than in men is patience. It is indeed a virtue in a tournament Poker game. The patience to wait for an open seat in a desirable game at which you have a legitimate chance to win as opposed to jumping into the first game that becomes available. The patience to wait for Hands you can play from a position of strength instead of anxiously attacking whatever cards you're dealt. Patience distinguishes *great* Poker Goddesses from delightful Poker prey. Of course, the best male pro players know the value of patience, too! As a woman, I must confess, I have a distinct distaste for going for an opponent's jugular merely to prove supremacy. I want the applause. The stature is more important to me than the power. So the excitement of the competition, to me, is more important than tearing somebody apart when you win and they lose.

What is the best advice you could give other women who want to challenge — and best — their male counterparts in Poker?

First and foremost, do your homework! Read and practice as suggested earlier. Second, play at a level at which you are well capitalized so you are confident. When you sit down at a Poker game, play at a level you can afford. View your Poker game as an income opportunity. Look at it in the same professional way you would at your regular job. Strive to be the best you can be. This is advice to be used against anybody, not just men. Use it whether you're playing against a man, a woman, a pedagogue, a Poker pro, a retiree, a mogul, or a munchkin!

Wendeen, why do you love Poker so much?

Poker is the one hobby that has kept my attention — and kept it intensely! It's a different experience every time I've been to a table in a Poker room, with an unending number of possible ways to conquer a tournament or a live game. Poker intellectually challenges. It's dangerous, character building, and above all, it's gratifying as a winner. You can't help but be charged up in a Poker game when the cards are cooperating. But if you truly care about the game, and I do, you will find that it tests your ability to put it all together.

- ♣ ♦ ♥ ♠ -

BEATING
LAS VEGAS

You've read the book! You've seen the movie! You've honed your Poker skills to a level that leaves your fellow Goddesses quaking with a white-knuckled mixture of fear and envy. You smartly decide it's time to take the show out of the kitchen and on the road — and smartly because you know you're ready to try your hand at something bigger, more exhilarating.

That road trip to the world of professional Poker playing leads generally in one of two directions, gals. It winds down the East Coast to the legendary shoreline of New Jersey, or way out West, through the desert to the City of Sin, Las Vegas.

Casino trips come complete with all the glitz, pageantry, and excitement of a Hollywood film. Just be aware of the rules. Know them before you set foot in the casino. And know that you've taken a big step away from friendly Poker games. You won't be playing with your pennies and nickels here.

In casinos, a Goddess buys colored Poker chips from the House to use in lieu of actual printed money, and then turns those chips back in for the real deal when ready to cash out — hopefully for more than when she started!

Las Vegas casinos use a standard color code for chips, with each color representing a different monetary value. The chips are:

♣ White = $1
♦ Red = $5
♥ Blue = $10
♠ Green = $25
♣ Black = $100
♦ Purple = $500

Many regular visitors to casinos are given 'Comps': complimentary drinks, gift certificates to specialty shops within the hotel, meals, and even room stays. Additionally, most casinos have their own websites, which offer a plethora of information on room rates, guest services, and the games they offer. The following is a comprehensive list of casinos located in both Atlantic City, New Jersey, and Las Vegas, Nevada.

Happy winning, ladies!

ATLANTIC CITY CASINOS

BALLY'S PARK PLACE CASINO & TOWER
Boardwalk & Park Place
Atlantic City, NJ 08401
(609)340-2000
(800)225-5977

CAESAR'S ATLANTIC CITY HOTEL CASINO
2100 Pacific Avenue
Atlantic City, NJ 08401
(609)348-4411
(800)524-2867

CLARIDGE CASINO HOTEL
Boardwalk & Park Place
Atlantic City, NJ 08401
(609)340-3400
(800)257-8585

THE ATLANTIC CITY HILTON
Boston & Pacific Avenues
Atlantic City, NJ 08401
(609)340-7100
(800)257-8677

HARRAH'S CASINO HOTEL
1725 Brigantine Blvd.
Atlantic City, NJ 08401
(609)441-5000
(800)2-HARRAH
(800)336-6378

RESORTS CASINO HOTEL
1133 Boardwalk (at North Carolina
Avenue)
Atlantic City, NJ 08401
(609)344-6000

SANDS HOTEL & CASINO
S. Indiana Ave & Brighton Park
Atlantic City, NJ 08401
(609)441-4000
(800)257-8580

SHOWBOAT CASINO HOTEL
Boardwalk & Delaware Ave
Atlantic City, NJ 08401
(609)343-4000
(800)621-0200

TROPICANA CASINO
Brighton Ave and Boardwalk
Atlantic City, NJ 08401
(609)340-4000
(800)257-6227

TRUMP PLAZA HOTEL & CASINO
Boardwalk & Mississippi Ave
Atlantic City, NJ 08401
(609)441-6000
(800)677-7378

TRUMP MARINA CASINO RESORT
Huron Ave & Brigantine Blvd
Atlantic City, NJ 08401
(609)441-2000
(800)777-1177

TRUMP TAJ MAHAL CASINO RESORT
1000 Virginia Ave (at Boardwalk)
Atlantic City, NJ 08401
(609)449-1000
(800)825-8786

LAS VEGAS CASINOS

ALADDIN RESORT & CASINO
3667 Las Vegas Blvd South
Las Vegas, NV 89107
(877)333-WISH
reservations@alladincasino.com

ARIZONA CHARLIE'S WEST
740 S. Decatur Blvd
Las Vegas, NV 89109
(800)342-2696
hotel@az.com

AZTEC GOLD
2200 Las Vegas South
Las Vegas, NV 89104
(702)385-4566

BALLY'S LAS VEGAS
3645 La Vegas Blvd South
Las Vegas, NV 89109-4307
(800)-7BALLYS
ballysguestservices@ballysiv.com

BARBARY COAST HOTEL & CASINO
3595 Las Vegas Blvd South
Las Vegas, NV 89109
(888)227-2279

BARCELONA HOTEL & CASINO
5011 East Craig Road
Las Vegas, NV 89115
(800)223-6330

BINION'S HORSESHOE
128 E. Fremont Street
Las Vegas, NV 89109
(800)622-6468
reservations@ivcm.com

BOULDER STATION
4111 Boulder Highway
Las Vegas, NV 89121
(800)683-7777

CAESAR'S PALACE
3570 Las Vegas Blvd
Las Vegas, NV 89109
(800)634-6661

CALIFORNIA HOTEL CASINO
12 Ogden Ave
Las Vegas, NV 89101
(800)634-6255

CASINO ROYALE HOTEL
3411 Las Vegas South
Las Vegas, NV 89109
(800)854-7666

CIRCUS CIRCUS HOTEL/CASINO/LAS VEGAS
2880 Las Vegas Blvd South
Las Vegas, NV 89109
(877)2-CIRCUS
(244-7287)

EL CORTEZ HOTEL & CASINO
600 East Fremont Street
Las Vegas, NV 89101
(800)634-6703

EXCALIBUR HOTEL/CASINO
3850 Las Vegas Blvd South
Las Vegas, NV 89109
(877)750-5464
info@excaliburcasino.com

FITZGERALDS CASINO/HOTEL
301 Fremont Street
Las Vegas, NV 89101
(800)274-LUCK

FLAMINGO HILTON LAS VEGAS
3555 Las Vegas Blvd South
Las Vegas, NV 89109
(800)732-2111

FOUR QUEENS
202 Fremont Street
Las Vegas, NV 89109
(800)634-6045

FRONTIER HOTEL
3120 Las Vegas Blvd South
Las Vegas, NV 89109
(800)634-6966

GOLD COAST
4000 West Flamingo Road
Las Vegas, NV 89103
(702)367-7111
(800)311-5334

GOLDEN SPIKE HOTEL & CASINO
400 East Ogden Ave
Las Vegas, NV 89101
(800)634-6703
(702)384-8444

GOLDEN GATE HOTEL & CASINO
1 Fremont Street
Las Vegas, NV 89101
(800)426-0521
(702)382-3510

HARD ROCK HOTEL & CASINO
4455 Paradise Road
Las Vegas, NV 89109
(800)HRD-ROCK
(702)693-5000

HARRAH'S CASINO LAS VEGAS
(800)634-6765
www.harrahs.com

HOLIDAY INN CASINO BOARDWALK
3750 West Sahara Ave
Las Vegas, NV 89117
(800)635-4581
(702)256-3766

HOLY COW! CASINO, CAFÉ & BREWERY
2423 Las Vegas Blvd South
Las Vegas, NV 89104
(702)732-2697

HOTEL SAN REMO
(800)522-7366

HOWARD JOHNSON HOTEL & CASINO
3111West Tropicana Ave
Las Vegas, NV 89103
(702)798-1111

IMPERIAL PALACE HOTEL & CASINO
3535 Las Vegas Blvd South
Las Vegas, NV 89101
(702)794-3114
(800)634-6441

JACKIE GAUGHAN'S PLAZA
1 South Main Street
Las Vegas, NV 89101
(702)386-2345
(800)634-6575

KLONDIKE HOTEL & CASINO
5191 Las Vegas Blvd South
Las Vegas, NV 89119
(702)739-9351

LADY LUCK LAS VEGAS
206 North 3rd Street
Las Vegas, NV 89101
(702)477-3000
(800)523-9582

LAS VEGAS CLUB HOTEL & CASINO
18 Fremont Street
Las Vegas, NV 89101
(702)385-1664

LAS VEGAS HILTON
3000 Paradise Road
Las Vegas, NV 89109
(800)732-7117

LONGHORN HOTEL/CASINO
5288 Boulder Highway
Las Vegas, NV 89122
(702)435-9170

LUXOR HOTEL CASINO
3900 Las Vegas Blvd South
Las Vegas, NV 89101
(702)262-4555
(800)288-1000

MAHONEY'S SILVER NUGGET CASINO
240 North Las Vegas Blvd
Las Vegas, NV 89109
(702)399-1111

MAIN STREET STATION CASINO & HOTEL
200 North Main Street
Las Vegas, NV 89101
(702)387-1896
(800)465-0711

MANDALAY BAY RESORT & CASINO
3950 Las Vegas Blvd South
Las Vegas, NV 89119
(702)736-3612
(877)632-7000

MGM GRAND HOTEL/CASINO
3799 Las Vegas Blvd South
Las Vegas, NV 89109
(702)891-7777
(800)929-1111

MONTE CARLO RESORT & CASINO
3770 Las Vegas Blvd South
Las Vegas, NV 89109
(702)730-7777
(800)311-8999

NEVADA PALACE HOTEL & CASINO
5255 Boulder Highway
Las Vegas, NV 89122
(702)898-8258
(800)637-5777

NEW YORK - NEW YORK HOTEL & CASINO
3790 Las Vegas Blvd South
Las Vegas, NV 89109
(702)740-6625
(800)693-6763

PALACE STATION
2411 West Sahara Ave
Las Vegas, NV 89102
(702)367-2401
(800)634-3101

PARIS LAS VEGAS CASINO RESORT
Flamingo Road
Las Vegas, NV 89109
(877)796-2096

QUALITY INN
377 East Flamingo Road
Las Vegas, NV 89109
(702)733-7777
(800)634-3101

RIO SUITE HOTEL & CASINO
3700 West Flamingo Road
Las Vegas, NV 89103
(702)252-7600
(800)888-1808

RIVIERA HOTEL & CASINO
2901 Las Vegas Blvd South
Las Vegas, NV 89109
(702)794-9424
(800)634-6753

ROYAL HOTEL/CASINO
99 Convention Drive
Las Vegas, NV 89109
(702)735-6117
(800)634-6118

SAM BOYD'S CALIFORNIA HOTEL & CASINO
12 East Ogden Ave
Las Vegas, NV 89101
(702)385-1222
(800)634-6460

SAM'S TOWN HOTEL & GAMBLING HALL
511 Boulder Highway
Las Vegas, NV 89122
(702)454-8148
(800)634-6371

SANDS HOTEL & CASINO
3355 Las Vegas Blvd South
Las Vegas, NV 89109
(702)414-1000

SANTA FE HOTEL & CASINO
4949 North Rancho Drive
Las Vegas, NV 89130
(702)658-4900
(800)872-6823

SASSY SALLY'S
32 Fremont Street
Las Vegas, NV 89101
(702)382-5777

SHERATON DESERT INN RESORT & CASINO
3145 Las Vegas Blvd South
Las Vegas, NV 89109
(702)733-4580

**SHOWBOAT HOTEL, CASINO & BOWLING
CENTER**
2800 Fremont Street
Las Vegas, NV 89104
(702)385-9190
(800)826-2800

SILVER CITY CASINO
3001 Las Vegas Blvd South
Las Vegas, NV 89109
(702)732-4152

SILVERTON HOTEL/CASINO & RV RESORT
333 West Baltimore Ave
Las Vegas, NV 89102
(702)263-7777
(800)588-7711

SLOTS-A-FUN
2880 Las Vegas Blvd South
Las Vegas, NV 89109
(702)734-0410

STARDUST RESORT & CASINO
3000 Las Vegas Blvd South
Las Vegas, NV 89109
(800)634-6757

TEXAS STATION GAMBLING HALL & RESORT
Las Vegas, NV 89101
(702)631-1055
(800)654-8888

THE GOLDEN NUGGET HOTEL & CASINO
129 Fremont Street
Las Vegas, NV 89101
(702)385-7111
(800)634-3454

THE MIRAGE
3400 Las Vegas Blvd South
Las Vegas, NV 89101
(702)792-4888
(800)800-627-6667

THE ORLEANS HOTEL & CASINO
4500 West Tropicana Ave
Las Vegas, NV 89103
(702)365-7111
(800)675-ORLEANS

THE VENETIAN RESORT
3355 Las Vegas Blvd South
Las Vegas, NV 89109
(702)733-5000
(888)283-6423

TREASURE ISLAND AT THE MIRAGE
3300 Las Vegas Blvd South
Las Vegas, NV 89109
(702)894-7111
(800)944-7444

TROPICANA RESORT & CASINO
3801 Las Vegas Blvd South
Las Vegas, NV 89109
(702)739-2222
(800)822-TROP

VACATION VILLAGE HOTEL/CASINO
6711 Las Vegas Blvd South
Las Vegas, NV 89119
(702)897-1700
(800)338-0609

WESTERN HOTEL & BINGO PARLOR
899 Fremont Street
Las Vegas, NV 89101
(702)384-4620
(800)634-6703

WESTWARD-HO HOTEL & CASINO
2900 Las Vegas Blvd South
Las Vegas, NV 89109
(702)731-2900
(800)634-6803

Appendix

While playing Poker can be profitable, overall it is meant to be enjoyed. It shouldn't ruin lives, which, sadly, gambling does every day. So ladies, please don't bet the family silver or your mortgage payment on a sure hand. As in all things, moderation is the key!

As part of our commitment to responsible gambling, we enclose the following contact information for Gamblers Anonymous. According to a GA spokeswoman, more than 30,000 men and women are estimated to regularly attend their meetings in the United States alone (but since GA doesn't keep records in its commitment to anonymity, this is just a rough guess). GA has offices in over 30 countries around the world. Attendance is anonymous, and help is just a phone call away. GA can be contacted at:

GAMBLERS ANONYMOUS
INTERNATIONAL SERVICE OFFICE

PO Box 17173
Los Angeles, CA 90017
(213)386-8789
(213)386-0030 (Fax)
www.gamblersanonymous.org (website)
isomain@gamblersanonymous.org (email)

By logging onto the website or calling the above number, you will find a local meeting in your area or hometown. If you or someone you love has a gambling problem, please contact Gamblers Anonymous for help.

A good Poker player is a responsible card player. Be responsible to your children, your family, your friends, and above all, yourself.

- ♣ ♦ ♥ ♠ -

Acknowledgements

The writers wish to thank the following, and are grateful for their support and encouragement:

> June Clark, the best damn book agent on the planet.
> 'Jacks are Wild' Jack David, a true King among the Queens of Poker.
> Wendeen Eolis and Tina Napolitano.
> Lovey Norris, Rachel Runge, and Phyllis Solomon, the three best grandmothers ever. Thank you for passing your passion for writing and the talent in your blood

down one generation to us. We'll love you for that gift — and many, many others — forever.

Our grandfathers, the Original Card Shark, 'Tonto' Toufic Solomon, and beloved 'Grampy' Wallace Runge.

Nicholas and Stacia Van Vleet.

John & Katherine Muir, great and trusted friends.

The wonderful 'Judy Beauty,' Judith Gagnon, for creating a safe, immortal haven for writers in the Merrimac Valley.

All our friends in The Essex Writers' Guild/Phoenix Writers and The Berkshire Banquet.

Tim Dudley, without whom very little Poker would have been played over the years.

Sue Mead, the epitome of inspiration.

Our many editors, publishers, and associates 'in the business' who were never too busy to give us the time of day — you know who you are.

The courageous men and women of Moonbase Alpha on *Space:1999.*

The crew of the Starship *Voyager.* Jeri Taylor, *Voyager's* talented creator who took us under her wings; Robert Beltran, Tim Russ, Ethan John Phillips, Bob Picardo, the lovely Roxann Dawson, Garrett Wang, and especially Robbie McNeill and Kate Mulgrew. Thank you for taking us with you on your voyage to the end of the galaxy and back.

And Buggy, Bear, Tommy, Itsy, Eleanor, Monster, Tuna, Mesquina, and the late Maya, beloved cats who sat on our laps and both aggravated and charmed us to no end during the writing of this book.